# WISCONSIN'S GHOSTLY LEGENDS

Other Titles by Scott Bowser:

Gein

The Ed Gein Chronicles

The Travelers Guide to Ed Gein

All are available on Amazon and Barnes & Noble.

© **2024 by Scott Bowser**

All rights reserved. No part of this book may be reproduced, stored in a retrieval system, or transmitted in any form or by any means without the prior written permission of the publisher except by a reviewer who may quote brief passages in a review to be printed in a newspaper, magazine or journal.

# TABLE OF CONTENT

FORWARD ................................................................................................ v

**CHAPTER 1**: ........................................................................................... 1
   THE PFISTER HOTEL ........................................................................ 1

**CHAPTER 2:** ........................................................................................... 6
   THE BRUMDER MANSION BED & BREAKFAST ....................... 6

**CHAPTER 3:** ......................................................................................... 11
   SUMMERWIND MANSON ............................................................. 11

**CHAPTER 4:** ......................................................................................... 17
   THE OLD BARABOO INN ............................................................... 17

**CHAPTER 5:** ......................................................................................... 23
   MARIBEL CAVES HOTEL ............................................................... 23

**CHAPTER 6:** ......................................................................................... 29
   THE GRAND OPERA HOUSE ......................................................... 29

**CHAPTER 7:** ......................................................................................... 35
   THE SHEBOYGAN ASYLUM ......................................................... 35

**CHAPTER 8:** ......................................................................................... 41
   THE KARSTEN HOTEL .................................................................... 41

**CHAPTER 9:** ......................................................................................... 47
THE WAUSHARA HISTORICAL SOCIETY MUSEUM & OLD JAIL
.................................................................................................................. 47

**CHAPTER 10:** ....................................................................................... 54
THE EAGLES CLUB ................................................................................ 54

**CHAPTER 11:** ....................................................................................... 60

| | |
|---|---|
| BLOODY BRIDE BRIDGE | 60 |
| **CHAPTER 12:** | **66** |
| THE OCTAGON HOUSE | 66 |
| **CHAPTER 13:** | **72** |
| DARTFORD CEMETERY | 72 |
| **CHAPTER 14:** | **79** |
| THE RED GYM | 79 |
| **CHAPTER 15:** | **86** |
| FOREST HOME CEMETERY | 86 |
| **CHAPTER 16:** | **94** |
| THE OLD WADE HOUSE | 94 |
| **CHAPTER 17:** | **102** |
| THE FIRST WARD SCHOOLHOUSE | 102 |
| **CHAPTER 18:** | **111** |
| THE HOAN BRIDGE | 111 |
| **CHAPTER 19:** | **118** |
| THE MASONIC TEMPLE | 118 |
| **CHAPTER 20:** | **125** |
| THE MILWAUKEE COURTHOUSE | 125 |
| **CHAPTER 21:** | **132** |
| BROADHEAD MANOR | 132 |
| **ABOUT THE AUTHOR** | **140** |
| **OTHER BOOKS BY SCOTT BOWSER** | **141** |

# FORWARD

## WHY WISCONSIN IS SO HAUNTED: AN EXPLORATION OF THE STATE'S PARANORMAL LEGACY

Wisconsin, known for its rolling hills, dense forests, and picturesque lakes, might not seem like an obvious hotspot for paranormal activity. Yet, the state is home to a wealth of haunted locations, each with its own chilling story. From historic mansions and ancient cemeteries to abandoned asylums and old inns, Wisconsin's haunted sites offer a glimpse into the supernatural side of this Midwestern state. But what makes Wisconsin such a haven for ghostly phenomena? Let's explore the historical, cultural, and geographical factors that contribute to Wisconsin's rich tapestry of hauntings.

### Historical Significance and Tragic Events

One of the key reasons Wisconsin is so haunted is its complex and often tragic history. The state's past is marked by numerous events and conditions that have left their mark on its landscape and its people. Historic buildings, including old hotels, mansions, and asylums, are frequently sites of paranormal activity, often linked to the individuals who lived or died there.

Take, for instance, the **Pfister Hotel** in Milwaukee. Opened in 1893, the hotel has been the site of numerous ghost sightings, including reports of Charles Pfister, the hotel's founder. The grandeur and historical significance of such buildings create an atmosphere ripe for lingering spirits. These sites often carry the energy of their past inhabitants, creating a backdrop for paranormal experiences.

Similarly, the **Maribel Caves Hotel** and its remote, abandoned state contribute to its haunted reputation. The hotel's closure and subsequent decay have created an environment where the spirits of former guests and staff may linger. The tragic and mysterious history surrounding these places often leaves a residual energy that can be sensed by the living.

## Cultural Beliefs and Folklore

Wisconsin's cultural and ethnic diversity has also played a role in shaping its haunted reputation. The state's population includes descendants of various European immigrants, each bringing their own folklore, superstitions, and beliefs about the afterlife. These cultural elements have influenced local ghost stories and paranormal lore.

For example, the **Brumder Mansion** in Milwaukee, with its early 20th-century design and its stories of ghostly apparitions, reflects the cultural attitudes and beliefs of its time. Such stories are often passed down through generations, contributing to the mansion's haunted reputation. The blending of cultural beliefs about spirits and the afterlife creates a rich tapestry of ghostly legends throughout the state.

Additionally, local folklore and urban legends, such as those surrounding **Bloody Bride Bridge** in Stevens Point, are influenced by the state's cultural narratives. These stories often reflect deeper fears and societal anxieties, which can manifest as paranormal phenomena.

## Geographical and Environmental Factors

The geographical and environmental features of Wisconsin also contribute to its haunted reputation. The state's dense forests, remote locations, and expansive cemeteries provide a perfect setting for ghost stories. The natural landscape often enhances the eerie atmosphere of haunted sites, making them feel more isolated and unsettling.

The **Dartford Cemetery** in Green Lake, with its ancient graves and overgrown vegetation, is a prime example of how the environment can contribute to a location's haunted reputation. The cemetery's history, combined with its atmospheric setting, makes it a focal point for paranormal activity.

Similarly, the **Old Baraboo Inn**, with its historic and somewhat dilapidated condition, provides an ideal environment for ghostly encounters. The inn's connection to notorious figures like Al Capone adds to its mystique, while the building's age and condition create an atmosphere conducive to paranormal experiences.

## Historical Buildings and Abandoned Sites

Many of Wisconsin's haunted locations are historic buildings and abandoned sites. These structures often have long histories of use and occupancy, making them ripe for ghostly activity. The decay and abandonment of these sites can create an environment where spirits are thought to linger, trapped in the remnants of their former lives.

The **Summer Wind Mansion** near Elkhart Lake, once a grand estate, is now known for its ghostly legends. The mansion's abandonment and subsequent deterioration have only added to its haunted reputation. Visitors report ghostly sightings and unexplained disturbances, which are often linked to the mansion's past inhabitants.

Likewise, the **Sheboygan Asylum**, with its history of mental health care and its abandonment, is a significant site for paranormal activity. The asylum's history of mistreatment and neglect contributes to its haunted reputation, with reports of eerie encounters and ghostly apparitions from former patients and staff.

## Tragic Events and Ghost Stories

Tragic events and untimely deaths often leave a significant imprint on the places where they occurred. Wisconsin's haunted locations frequently have a history of such events, which can contribute to their paranormal activity. Ghost stories often arise from these tragic occurrences, creating a narrative that adds to the location's haunted reputation.

The **Waushara County Historical Museum and Old Jail** in Wautoma, for example, is associated with notorious criminal Ed Gein. The site's dark history and connection to a notorious figure create a backdrop for ghostly legends and paranormal encounters. Similarly, the **Old Wade House** in Greenbush, with its history as a stagecoach inn, has been the site of ghostly activity linked to traveller's former inhabitants.

## The Allure of the Unknown

Finally, the allure of the unknown plays a significant role in Wisconsin's haunted reputation. The state's numerous ghost stories and paranormal legends captivate the imagination and draw people to its haunted locations. The excitement and curiosity surrounding these sites often lead to increased reports of ghostly encounters and paranormal activity.

The **Eagles Club** in Milwaukee and the **Karsten Hotel** in Kewaunee are examples of locations that attract paranormal enthusiasts and investigators. The intrigue and fascination with the supernatural contribute to the growing lore surrounding these sites, perpetuating their haunted reputations.

# CHAPTER 1

## THE PFISTER HOTEL

### (Milwaukee)

The Pfister Hotel in Milwaukee, Wisconsin, is an architectural gem with a storied past, rich with history and an abundance of ghostly tales. Built in 1893 by businessman Guido Pfister and his son, Charles, this grand hotel has hosted a variety of notable guests over the years, from presidents and dignitaries to celebrities and sports teams. However, it's not just the living who seem to have an affinity for this historic hotel; numerous reports of paranormal activity have cemented its reputation as one of the most haunted hotels in America.

The Pfister Hotel's haunting lore begins with its founder, Charles Pfister. Many believe that Charles' spirit never left the building and that he continues to watch over the hotel he cherished so dearly. Guests and staff alike have reported seeing a man fitting Charles' description—dressed in a Victorian-era suit—wandering the halls and checking on the hotel's operations. This ghostly figure is often seen on the grand staircase or near the lobby, where he appears to be ensuring everything is in order. Some say they've felt an inexplicable presence while alone, only to turn and see a fleeting glimpse of Charles before he disappears.

But the hauntings at the Pfister Hotel are not limited to the apparition of Charles Pfister. Over the years, numerous guests have reported a variety of paranormal experiences, particularly those staying on the upper floors. One of the most common occurrences is the sudden malfunctioning of electronic devices. TVs and radios are known to turn on and off by themselves, often at full volume, startling unsuspecting guests in the middle of the night. Lights flicker without explanation, and some have reported their electronic devices behaving erratically or even being drained of power completely, only to return to normal once they leave the hotel.

Another frequent report involves disembodied voices and strange noises. Guests have heard footsteps in empty hallways, knocks on their doors with no one on the other side, and even the faint sound of children playing when no children are present. These occurrences are often accompanied by cold spots—areas of inexplicable chill that can send shivers down one's spine despite the room's ambient temperature.

Athletes from visiting baseball teams have provided some of the most publicized accounts of the paranormal activity at the Pfister

Hotel. Players from various Major League Baseball teams have reported strange experiences, ranging from unsettling noises to more direct encounters. Some have been so disturbed by these occurrences that they refuse to stay at the hotel altogether, opting for alternative accommodations whenever their team is in town to play the Milwaukee Brewers. Notably, in 2001, Adrian Beltre, a former third baseman, shared a chilling story of waking up to heavy furniture in his room having been moved overnight while he slept. He was so shaken that he vowed never to stay at the Pfister again.

In addition to these ghostly tales, the Pfister Hotel has a rich history that adds depth to its mystique. The hotel's design, an opulent blend of Romanesque Revival architecture, features marble accents, elaborate chandeliers, and detailed woodwork, all of which contribute to its majestic and somewhat eerie atmosphere. The grand lobby, with its high ceilings and elegant decor, exudes a timeless charm that seems to transcend the decades. This historical ambiance might also play a role in the hotel's paranormal activity, as it seems to evoke a strong sense of the past and its lingering spirits.

The Pfister Hotel embraces its haunted reputation, offering ghost tours and encouraging guests to share their paranormal experiences. The hotel's staff, many of whom have their own stories of eerie encounters, are often willing to discuss the ghostly happenings and point out locations within the hotel known for unusual activity. Despite—or perhaps because of—its haunted reputation, the Pfister continues to be a popular destination for travelers seeking both luxury and a brush with the supernatural.

One particularly intriguing aspect of Pfister's ghost story is how it has been woven into the fabric of Milwaukee's cultural narrative. Local legends and personal anecdotes contribute to a rich tapestry of ghostly lore, making the Pfister Hotel a must-visit location for those interested in the paranormal. The hotel's inclusion in ghost tours and its frequent mention in articles and books about haunted places in America only add to its allure.

In conclusion, the Pfister Hotel in Milwaukee, Wisconsin, stands as a testament to both historical grandeur and supernatural intrigue. Its beautiful architecture and luxurious amenities make it a premier destination for travelers, while its ghostly legends attract paranormal enthusiasts and skeptics alike. Whether you believe in ghosts or not, the stories surrounding the Pfister Hotel add an undeniable layer of fascination and mystery to this iconic Milwaukee landmark. Visitors come for comfort and elegance, but they often leave with stories of the unexplained, contributing to the ever-growing legend of the Pfister Hotel's haunted legacy.

Pfister Hotel

## CONCLUSION

Wisconsin's haunted reputation is a product of its complex history, diverse cultural influences, and unique geographical features. The state's historic buildings, abandoned sites, and tragic events all contribute to its rich tapestry of ghost stories and paranormal activity. From the opulent Pfister Hotel to the eerie Summer Wind Mansion, Wisconsin offers a diverse array of haunted locations that continue to captivate and intrigue those drawn to the supernatural. Whether influenced by cultural beliefs, historical events, or the allure of the unknown, Wisconsin's haunted legacy is an enduring part of the state's mystique.

# CHAPTER 2

## THE BRUMDER MANSION BED & BREAKFAST

### (Milwaukee)

The Brumder Mansion in Milwaukee, Wisconsin, is not only a beautiful example of Victorian architecture but also a hotspot for paranormal activity. Built in 1910 by George Brumder, a prominent German immigrant and Milwaukee businessman, this historic mansion has seen numerous occupants and has become well-known for its ghostly residents. Over the years, it has operated as a private residence, a boarding house, and a bed and breakfast, with each phase of its history contributing to its haunted reputation.

The mansion's ghost stories begin with its very first owner, George Brumder, whose presence is still felt by many who visit. George Brumder was a significant figure in Milwaukee, known for his contributions to the city's development and his success in the publishing industry. It is believed that his spirit continues to watch over the mansion he built, ensuring it remains a place of beauty and elegance. Guests and staff have reported seeing a man in period clothing, thought to be George himself, roaming the halls or appearing in mirrors. This figure is often described as benevolent and watchful, more a guardian than a typical haunting presence.

One of the most frequently reported paranormal phenomena at the Brumder Mansion involves unexplained noises. Guests often hear footsteps on the stairs, doors opening and closing on their own, and disembodied voices engaged in conversation. These sounds usually occur when no one else is around, adding to the eerie atmosphere of the mansion. One notable incident involved a guest hearing the distinct sound of a piano playing late at night, only to find the music room empty and the piano lid closed.

The Blue Room, one of the mansion's guest rooms, is particularly noted for its paranormal activity. Many guests who have stayed in the Blue Room have reported feeling an unsettling presence as if someone were watching them. Some have even claimed to see shadowy figures moving about the room. The presence is often accompanied by cold spots and sudden temperature drops that have no logical explanation. One guest recounted waking up in the middle of the night to see a woman dressed in early 20th-century clothing standing at the foot of the bed, only for the figure to vanish when they turned on the light.

Another room known for its ghostly activity is the Gold Suite. This luxurious room has been the site of numerous strange occurrences, including objects moving on their own and lights flickering without cause. Guests have also reported hearing the sound of someone pacing back and forth outside the door, even when the hallway is empty. The ghostly presence in the Gold Suite is often described as more playful than menacing, leading some to speculate that it might be the spirit of a child.

The basement of the Brumder Mansion is another area where paranormal activity is frequently reported. This part of the mansion, once used for various domestic purposes, now houses a theater and a bar area. Many people have reported feeling an intense, almost oppressive atmosphere in the basement as if they are not alone. Some have seen apparitions in the basement, including a woman in a long dress who appears and disappears suddenly. There are also reports of hearing whispers and seeing shadowy figures darting around the basement's dark corners.

Staff members at the Brumder Mansion have their own ghost stories to share. One housekeeper recounted an experience of cleaning a room when she felt a cold breeze pass by despite the windows being closed. She turned to see a figure out of the corner of her eye, but when she looked directly, no one was there. Another staff member reported setting up for a breakfast service early in the morning and hearing footsteps approaching from behind, only to find herself alone when she turned around.

The mansion's paranormal reputation extends to its garden as well. Visitors have reported seeing ghostly figures wandering the grounds, especially during twilight and late at night. These apparitions are often described as looking lost or searching for something. The garden, with its tranquil paths and historic ambiance, seems to be a place where the past and present intersect, allowing these spirits to make themselves known.

One of the more famous ghost stories associated with the Brumder Mansion involves a séance conducted by a group of paranormal investigators. The séance reportedly resulted in contact with multiple spirits, who communicated through knocks, table movements, and even direct voice messages. The investigators claimed that they had made contact with a former resident of the mansion who was seeking closure on unresolved matters. The details of these communications were chilling and added credence to the mansion's haunted reputation.

Despite its haunted reputation, or perhaps because of it, the Brumder Mansion continues to operate as a bed and breakfast, drawing visitors who are curious about its history and its ghosts. The owners embrace the mansion's paranormal aspect, offering ghost tours and inviting paranormal investigators to explore the property. This openness to the supernatural has only increased the mansion's allure, making it a popular destination for those interested in the paranormal.

In conclusion, the Brumder Mansion in Milwaukee is a captivating blend of history and hauntings. Its beautiful Victorian architecture and luxurious interiors provide a striking backdrop for the many ghost stories that have emerged over the years. Whether it's the benevolent spirit of George Brumder, the mysterious woman in the Blue Room, or the playful presence in the Gold Suite, the mansion's ghostly residents add an extra layer of intrigue to this historic property. Visitors to the Brumder Mansion come for comfort and charm but often leave with tales of the unexplained, ensuring that the mansion's legacy as one of Milwaukee's most haunted locations endures.

# CHAPTER 3

## SUMMERWIND MANSON

### (West Bay Lake)

Summerwind Mansion, located on the shores of West Bay Lake in Wisconsin, is widely regarded as one of the most haunted locations in the United States. Built in the early 20th century, this once-grand mansion has a storied history filled with ghostly tales and paranormal phenomena that have intrigued and terrified visitors for decades.

The mansion's haunting reputation began with its construction in 1916 by Robert P. Lamont, a wealthy businessman who served as Secretary of Commerce under President Herbert Hoover. Lamont used Summerwind as a summer retreat for his family, but their time at the mansion was short-lived. According to legend, the Lamont family experienced numerous inexplicable occurrences during their stays, including strange noises, shadowy figures, and objects moving on their own. The most famous story involves Robert Lamont himself. One evening, while he was in the kitchen, he reportedly saw the apparition of a man materialize before him. Terrified, Lamont pulled out his pistol and fired two shots at the ghostly figure, but the bullets passed through it and lodged into a door behind where the apparition stood. The bullet holes are said to have remained in the door for years, serving as a chilling reminder of the encounter.

Following the Lamont family's departure, the mansion changed hands several times, with each new owner reporting similar supernatural activities. In the 1940s, the Keefer family purchased Summerwind, but their experiences were no less unsettling. The family reported hearing disembodied voices, seeing ghostly apparitions, and experiencing sudden drops in temperature. Despite their attempts to make the mansion a livable home, the hauntings proved too much, and they eventually abandoned the property.

In the 1970s, Summerwind gained national attention when it was purchased by Arnold and Ginger Hinshaw. The Hinshaws moved into the mansion with their six children, hoping to restore the once beautiful property. However, their time at Summerwind quickly turned into a nightmare. The family reported a wide range of paranormal phenomena, including ghostly apparitions, strange sounds, and objects moving on their own. Ginger Hinshaw recounted hearing organ music coming from the mansion's organ room, even though the instrument was known to be broken and incapable of producing sound.

One of the most terrifying incidents involved the discovery of a hidden room. While attempting to make renovations, Arnold Hinshaw found a small, concealed space behind a closet wall. Inside the hidden room, he discovered human remains, which he believed to be the source of the mansion's haunting. However, there is no official record of this discovery, and the truth behind the hidden room remains shrouded in mystery.

The hauntings took a severe toll on the Hinshaw family. Arnold Hinshaw reportedly suffered from severe mood swings and eventually had a mental breakdown. Ginger Hinshaw also experienced a nervous breakdown, and the couple eventually separated. Their experiences at Summerwind were documented in a book titled "The Carver Effect: A Paranormal Experience," written by Ginger's father, Raymond Bober, under the pseudonym Wolfgang Von Bober. In the book, Bober claimed to have communicated with a spirit named Jonathan Carver, an 18th-century explorer, who revealed that the mansion was built on sacred Native American land, leading to its haunted nature.

Following the Hinshaw family's departure, Summerwind remained abandoned for many years. It became a popular destination for thrill-seekers, paranormal investigators, and curiosity-driven tourists, all hoping to catch a glimpse of the mansion's ghostly inhabitants. Numerous investigations have been conducted at Summerwind, with many investigators reporting strange phenomena, including EVP (electronic voice phenomena) recordings, unexplained shadows, and sudden temperature drops.

One particularly well-known investigation was conducted by the Wisconsin Society for Psychic Research (WSPR) in the late 1980s. The team spent several nights at the mansion, capturing various pieces of evidence that suggested paranormal activity. They recorded strange noises, and voices and even captured photographs of shadowy figures. Their findings further solidified Summerwind's reputation as a haunted location.

Despite its haunted history, Summerwind's physical structure could not withstand the test of time. In 1988, a lightning strike ignited a fire that severely damaged the mansion, leaving it in ruins. The remaining structure was eventually demolished, and today, only the foundation and a few remnants of the mansion remain. However, even in its dilapidated state, Summerwind continues to attract those fascinated by its ghostly lore.

The tales of Summerwind's hauntings have continued to grow over the years, with many visitors reporting strange experiences even at the site of the ruins. Some claim to have seen ghostly figures wandering the grounds, while others report hearing disembodied voices and footsteps. The legend of the hidden room and its supposed human remains also persists, adding to the mansion's mystique.

One theory behind the hauntings at Summerwind is that the mansion was built on land sacred to Native Americans. Some believe that disturbing this land may have angered spirits who then haunted the property. Others suggest that the mansion's history of tragedy and misfortune—such as the Lamont family's experiences, the Keefer family's abandonment, and the Hinshaw family's breakdown—has left a residual energy that manifests as paranormal activity.

Regardless of the true cause, Summerwind remains one of Wisconsin's most infamous haunted locations. Its history of ghostly encounters, combined with the dramatic accounts from its former residents and investigators, has cemented its place in American paranormal lore. While the mansion itself no longer stands, its legacy continues to captivate and terrify those who dare to explore its haunted past.

In conclusion, Summerwind Mansion is a place where history and the supernatural intertwine. From its construction by Robert P. Lamont to the harrowing experiences of the Hinshaw family, the mansion has been the site of numerous ghostly encounters and unexplained phenomena. Even in ruins,

Summerwind's reputation as a haunted location endures, drawing the curious and the brave to its mysterious remnants. Whether one believes in ghosts or not, the stories of Summerwind Mansion offer a fascinating glimpse into the world of the paranormal and the enduring power of a good ghost story.

Summerwind Mansion

# CHAPTER 4

## THE OLD BARABOO INN

### (Baraboo)

The Old Baraboo Inn, located in Baraboo, Wisconsin, is a historic establishment known for its rich history, charming architecture, and reputation for being one of the most haunted places in the state. Built-in the late 19th century, this former saloon and brothel have been the site of numerous ghostly sightings and unexplained phenomena, attracting paranormal enthusiasts and curious visitors alike.

The history of the Old Baraboo Inn dates back to 1864 when it was established as a stop for travellers and workers in the area. Over the years, it became a popular gathering place for the locals, serving as a saloon and brothel. The inn's colourful past is filled with tales of Wild West-style brawls, illicit activities, and untimely deaths, which some believe have contributed to the building's haunted reputation.

One of the most well-known spirits said to haunt the Old Baraboo Inn is that of a woman named Mary, who was reportedly a madam during the inn's days as a brothel. According to local legend, Mary met a tragic end when she was murdered by a jealous lover. Her restless spirit is said to roam the inn, and many visitors and employees have reported seeing her ghostly figure, often described as a woman in period clothing, wandering the hallways and appearing in mirrors. Some have even claimed to feel a cold, eerie presence or hear the sound of a woman's voice when no one else is around.

Another frequently reported apparition is that of a man believed to be a former patron or worker at the inn. Descriptions of this ghost vary, but he is often seen wearing old-fashioned work clothes and is sometimes spotted sitting at the bar or in one of the inn's many rooms. This spirit is said to be mischievous, with reports of him moving objects, turning lights on and off, and even touching or pushing unsuspecting guests.

In addition to these well-known spirits, there have been numerous other sightings and unexplained events at the Old Baraboo Inn. Guests have reported seeing shadowy figures, hearing disembodied footsteps, and experiencing sudden drops in temperature. Some have even claimed to see objects levitating or moving on their own. These occurrences have led many to believe that the inn is a hotspot for paranormal activity.

One of the most famous paranormal investigations at the Old Baraboo Inn was conducted by the television show "Ghost Adventures" in 2017. During their investigation, the team captured several pieces of compelling evidence, including EVP (electronic voice phenomena) recordings of ghostly voices and unexplained noises. They also reported experiencing physical sensations, such as sudden cold spots and the feeling of being touched by unseen hands. The episode brought national attention to the inn's haunted reputation and further fueled interest in its ghostly inhabitants.

In addition to "Ghost Adventures," several other paranormal groups have investigated the Old Baraboo Inn, each reporting their own encounters with the supernatural. The Wisconsin Paranormal Investigators, for example, conducted an investigation in which they captured EVPs' shadowy figures on camera and experienced personal encounters with what they believed to be spirits. Their findings added to the growing body of evidence suggesting that the inn is indeed haunted.

The current owner of the Old Baraboo Inn, Brenda Chilson, has embraced the inn's haunted reputation and regularly hosts paranormal events and ghost tours. Chilson herself has experienced numerous unexplained occurrences since taking over the inn, including seeing apparitions, hearing disembodied voices, and witnessing objects moving on their own. She believes that the spirits are mostly friendly and sees the hauntings as a unique aspect of the inn's charm.

One particularly eerie event that Chilson recalls involves a group of visitors who were taking part in a ghost tour. As they were walking through the inn, several members of the group reported feeling a sudden, intense chill and seeing a shadowy figure darting across the hallway. Moments later, they heard the sound of a woman's voice whispering, "Get out." The experience left the visitors visibly shaken and further solidified the inn's reputation as a place of paranormal activity.

Another chilling account comes from a former employee who worked at the inn for several years. According to the employee, he often heard the sound of footsteps coming from empty rooms and saw doors opening and closing on their own. On one occasion, he claimed to have seen the apparition of a man standing behind the bar, only for the figure to vanish when he approached. The employee eventually left the job, citing the constant feeling of being watched and the numerous unsettling experiences as his reasons for leaving.

Despite its haunted reputation, the Old Baraboo Inn remains a popular destination for both locals and tourists. Many visitors come specifically for the chance to experience the paranormal, while others are drawn by the inn's historic charm and lively atmosphere.

The inn offers a variety of events and activities, including live music, themed parties, and, of course, ghost tours.

The ghost tours, in particular, have become a significant attraction, drawing visitors from across the country. These tours offer a chance to explore the inn's history and hear firsthand accounts of ghostly encounters. Participants often bring their own paranormal investigation equipment, such as EMF detectors and digital voice recorders, in hopes of capturing evidence of the supernatural. Many leave with chilling stories and a newfound belief in the paranormal.

In conclusion, the Old Baraboo Inn in Baraboo, Wisconsin, is a historic establishment with a haunted reputation that has captivated the imaginations of many. From its days as a saloon and brothel to its current status as a popular paranormal destination, the inn's history is filled with tales of ghostly apparitions, unexplained phenomena, and chilling encounters. Whether one believes in ghosts or not, the stories and experiences of those who have visited the Old Baraboo Inn offer a fascinating glimpse into the world of the supernatural and the enduring allure of haunted places. The inn continues to attract those curious about its ghostly past, and for those brave enough to visit, it promises an experience they won't soon forget.

The Old Baraboo Inn

# CHAPTER 5

## MARIBEL CAVES HOTEL

### (Maribel)

The Maribel Caves Hotel, also known as the "Hotel Hell," is a historic and eerie landmark in Maribel, Wisconsin. Nestled in the rolling hills of Manitowoc County, this once grand hotel now stands in ruins, attracting both history buffs and paranormal enthusiasts. Its hauntingly beautiful architecture and ghostly legends have made it a hotspot for those seeking to uncover the mysteries of the supernatural.

The Maribel Caves Hotel was built in 1900 by Charles and Emil Wittmann as a luxury resort. Designed in the Queen Anne style, the hotel featured elegant verandas, a grand ballroom, and luxurious accommodations. It quickly gained a reputation as a premier destination for the wealthy and elite, who came to enjoy the natural springs and scenic beauty of the area. However, the hotel's glory days were short-lived.

In 1915, a devastating fire broke out, reducing the grand structure to rubble. The hotel was partially rebuilt, but it never regained its former splendour. Over the years, it changed hands multiple times and served various purposes, including as a sanitarium and a nightclub. Each phase of its history added layers to the building's lore, with numerous tales of tragedy and mystery emerging.

One of the most enduring legends of the Maribel Caves Hotel is that it is haunted by the spirits of those who perished in the fire. According to local lore, several guests and staff members lost their lives in the blaze, and their restless spirits are said to roam the ruins still. Visitors have reported seeing apparitions of ghostly figures, hearing disembodied voices, and experiencing sudden drops in temperature. Some have even claimed to know the hotel engulfed in phantom flames, reliving the tragic event that led to its downfall.

Another chilling story associated with the Maribel Caves Hotel involves the notorious serial killer Ed Gein. While there is no historical evidence to support this claim, it is said that Gein frequented the hotel during its days as a sanitarium. According to the legend, Gein, who was known for his gruesome crimes in the 1950s, was a patient at the sanitarium and carried out some of his dark deeds in the hotel's basement. This connection to one of America's most infamous killers has only added to the hotel's sinister reputation.

The hotel's basement, in particular, is a focal point for many of the ghostly tales. It is said to be a hotbed of paranormal activity, with visitors reporting encounters with malevolent spirits and strange phenomena. Some have described seeing shadowy figures lurking in the corners, hearing unsettling noises, and feeling an overwhelming sense of dread. The basement's dark and claustrophobic atmosphere only heightens the fear and unease experienced by those who venture down there.

In addition to the spirits of the fire victims and the alleged connection to Ed Gein, the Maribel Caves Hotel is also rumoured to be haunted by the ghost of a former caretaker. According to the legend, the caretaker, who lived on the property, met a tragic end when he was crushed by a falling beam during one of the hotel's renovations. His spirit is said to linger in the ruins, watching over the place he once cared for. Visitors have reported seeing his apparition, dressed in old-fashioned work clothes, wandering the grounds and staring out from the windows.

Paranormal investigators and ghost hunters have been drawn to the Maribel Caves Hotel for years, hoping to capture evidence of the supernatural. Many have reported experiencing unexplainable phenomena, from eerie EVPs (electronic voice phenomena) to strange anomalies on video and photographic equipment. The hotel's reputation as a haunted location has been further cemented by these investigations, which often yield compelling, albeit chilling, results.

One of the most famous investigations took place in the early 2000s when a group of paranormal researchers spent the night at the Maribel Caves Hotel. Equipped with an array of ghost-hunting equipment, including EMF detectors, infrared cameras, and digital voice recorders, they set out to document the paranormal activity reported by so many. Throughout the night, they experienced a series of unexplainable events, including disembodied voices, sudden temperature drops, and the feeling of being watched. One of the most startling pieces of evidence they captured was an EVP recording of what appeared to be a woman's voice whispering, "Help me."

Despite its haunted reputation, the Maribel Caves Hotel remains a popular destination for those intrigued by the paranormal. The ruins, though dilapidated and overgrown, still exude an eerie charm that draws visitors from near and far. Many come to explore the grounds, hoping to catch a glimpse of a ghostly figure or experience the inexplicable phenomena that have been reported so frequently.

In recent years, there have been efforts to preserve and restore the Maribel Caves Hotel. Local historians and preservationists recognize the importance of maintaining this historic site, not only for its architectural significance but also for its place in the cultural fabric of the community. While the future of the hotel remains uncertain, its legacy as a haunted landmark is likely to endure.

The Maribel Caves Hotel is also a testament to the power of local legends and the enduring fascination with the paranormal. The stories and experiences shared by those who have visited the site contribute to a rich tapestry of folklore that continues to captivate the imagination. Whether one believes in ghosts or not, the tales of the Maribel Caves Hotel offer a glimpse into the human desire to connect with the past and explore the mysteries of the unknown.

In conclusion, the Maribel Caves Hotel in Maribel, Wisconsin, is a place steeped in history and haunted by a multitude of ghostly legends. From the tragic fire that claimed the lives of guests and staff to the alleged connection to serial killer Ed Gein, the hotel's dark past has left an indelible mark on its present. Paranormal investigators and curious visitors alike are drawn to the site, seeking to uncover the truth behind the ghostly apparitions and unexplained phenomena. As efforts to preserve the historic ruins continue, the Maribel Caves Hotel remains a fascinating and eerie destination for those intrigued by the supernatural.

Maribel Caves Hotel

# CHAPTER 6

## THE GRAND OPERA HOUSE

### (Oshkosh)

The Grand Opera House in Oshkosh, Wisconsin, stands as a beacon of historical and cultural significance, yet its reputation is shrouded in tales of ghostly encounters and paranormal phenomena. This majestic venue, built in 1883, has hosted countless performances, from operas and plays to concerts and community events. Despite its grandeur and contribution to the arts, the Grand Opera House is equally famous for its spectral residents, making it a focal point for ghost hunters and those fascinated by the supernatural.

The history of the Grand Opera House is rich and storied. Designed by prominent architect William Waters, the building was constructed at the height of Oshkosh's prosperity. Waters' vision was to create a premier entertainment venue that would rival the best theatres in the country. The opera house's Victorian design, complete with ornate decorations, intricate woodwork, and a stunning proscenium arch, made it an architectural marvel of its time.

Throughout the years, the Grand Opera House has seen numerous renovations and restorations to preserve its historical integrity. Despite these efforts, the building's age and the events it has witnessed have contributed to its reputation as one of Wisconsin's most haunted locations. Tales of ghostly apparitions, unexplained noises, and eerie occurrences have become an integral part of its lore, drawing both sceptics and believers to explore its haunted history.

One of the most frequently reported ghostly encounters at the Grand Opera House involves a mysterious figure known as "Percy." Percy is believed to be the spirit of a former stagehand who worked at the opera house during its early years. According to legend, Percy met a tragic end in a backstage accident, possibly involving the complex rigging system used to manage stage curtains and scenery. His restless spirit is said to linger in the theatre, often seen by staff and visitors alike.

Witnesses describe Percy as a shadowy figure who moves silently through the backstage area, occasionally appearing on the catwalks above the stage. His presence is often accompanied by a sudden drop in temperature and the faint smell of smoke, a chilling reminder of the fire that claimed his life. Some have reported hearing Percy's footsteps echoing in the empty theatre, as well as the sound of tools being used as if he continues to perform his duties from beyond the grave.

Another prominent ghostly resident of the Grand Opera House is known as "Emily." Emily is said to be the spirit of a young actress who performed at the theatre during the late 19th century. According to local lore, Emily was a rising star whose life was cut short under mysterious circumstances. Some believe she fell victim to foul play, while others suggest she succumbed to illness or heartbreak. Regardless of the cause, Emily's spirit is said to haunt the opera house, particularly the dressing rooms and the stage where she once performed.

Emily's ghost is often described as a beautiful young woman dressed in period attire. She is known to appear in mirrors, her reflection startling those who see her. Witnesses have also reported hearing Emily's voice, sometimes singing softly or reciting lines from her favourite roles. Her presence is said to be both comforting and melancholic as if she is still longing for the applause and adoration she received in life.

The Grand Opera House is also home to a spectral child, often referred to as "Tommy." Tommy's origins are less clear, but he is believed to be the spirit of a young boy who either lived near the opera house or was somehow connected to it. Some speculate that he may have been an orphan or a street child who found refuge in the theatre. Tommy's ghost is often seen playing in the balconies and the lobby, his laughter echoing through the halls.

Witnesses describe Tommy as a playful spirit, his presence marked by the sound of small footsteps and the occasional sighting of a young boy running through the theatre. He is known to interact with visitors, particularly children, who often report feeling a sense of companionship and playfulness when Tommy is near. Some have even claimed that toys and other objects left in the theatre are mysteriously moved or rearranged, as if by an unseen hand.

In addition to these individual spirits, there are numerous reports of general paranormal activity throughout the Grand Opera House. Many have experienced sudden cold spots, unexplained gusts of wind, and the feeling of being watched. Lights are known to flicker on and off, and doors have been observed opening and closing on their own. The sound of disembodied voices, music, and even the faint echoes of applause has been reported as if the theatre is still alive with the energy of past performances.

One of the most unsettling areas of the opera house is the basement, which houses the original dressing rooms and storage areas. This space is known for its oppressive atmosphere and is often avoided by staff and visitors. Many have reported feeling an overwhelming sense of dread and discomfort when venturing into the basement as if they are not alone. Some have even claimed to see shadowy figures darting through the darkness, adding to the sense of unease.

The Grand Opera House has attracted the attention of numerous paranormal investigators over the years. Teams equipped with advanced ghost-hunting equipment, including EMF detectors, thermal cameras, and EVP recorders, have conducted investigations in an attempt to capture evidence of the supernatural. These investigations have yielded intriguing results, including recordings of unexplained voices, photographic anomalies, and fluctuations in electromagnetic fields.

One particularly compelling piece of evidence was captured during an investigation by a local paranormal group. While conducting an EVP session on the stage, the team recorded a clear and distinct voice responding to their questions. The voice, believed to be that of Emily, stated, "I am here," and "Help me," sending chills through the investigators. This recording, along with other findings, has added to the growing body of evidence supporting the opera house's haunted reputation.

Despite its haunted history, the Grand Opera House remains a beloved cultural landmark in Oshkosh. The theatre continues to host performances and events, drawing audiences who appreciate its historical significance and architectural beauty. For many, the stories of ghostly encounters add to the allure of the venue, creating an atmosphere that is both enchanting and mysterious.

In conclusion, the Grand Opera House in Oshkosh, Wisconsin, is a place where history and the supernatural intertwine. From the tragic tales of Percy and Emily to the playful spirit of Tommy, the theatre is home to a rich tapestry of ghostly residents. The numerous reports of paranormal activity, coupled with the findings of investigators, have cemented its status as one of Wisconsin's most haunted locations. Whether one believes in ghosts or not, the stories and experiences of those who have encountered the spirits of the Grand Opera House offer a fascinating glimpse into the world of the supernatural and the enduring legacy of this historic venue.

Grand Opera House — Oshkosh, Wis.

# CHAPTER 7

## THE SHEBOYGAN ASYLUM

### (Sheboygan)

The Sheboygan Asylum, also known as the Sheboygan County Comprehensive Health Care Center, in Sheboygan, Wisconsin, has a history that is as unsettling as it is fascinating. Established in 1940, the asylum originally served as a psychiatric hospital, providing care for those with mental illnesses, developmental disabilities, and other conditions requiring long-term treatment. Over the decades, the facility has been the subject of numerous ghost stories and paranormal investigations, drawing attention to the eerie occurrences reported by both staff and visitors.

The institution's architecture, with its long, narrow hallways, high ceilings, and numerous wards, creates an atmosphere that can be quite intimidating. The building's design, typical of early 20th-century psychiatric hospitals, is inherently eerie, with its labyrinthine layout contributing to the sense of disorientation and unease. The institution was closed in the 1990s, and since then, it has become a magnet for ghost hunters and thrill-seekers, all hoping to catch a glimpse of the supernatural.

One of the most frequently reported paranormal occurrences at the Sheboygan Asylum is the sound of disembodied voices. Many visitors and paranormal investigators have claimed to hear voices echoing through the empty halls, often sounding distressed or agitated. These voices are sometimes heard as whispers, but there are also reports of loud, anguished cries that seem to come from nowhere. This auditory phenomenon is particularly common in the building's basement, which housed the facility's morgue and storage areas.

Another common report involves the appearance of shadowy figures. These apparitions are often seen out of the corner of the eye, darting quickly across hallways or peeking around corners. Some visitors have described seeing full-bodied apparitions, often dressed in period clothing typical of the asylum's operational years. These ghostly figures are usually seen in the patient wards and common areas, where they appear to go about their activities as if still alive.

The ghost of a nurse often referred to as "Nurse Betty," is one of the most well-known spirits said to haunt the Sheboygan Asylum. According to legend, Nurse Betty was a compassionate caregiver who tragically took her own life within the asylum. Her spirit is said to linger, continuing to care for the patients she once tended to. Witnesses have reported seeing a woman in a nurse's uniform walking the halls, her footsteps echoing in the silence. Some have even claimed to feel a comforting presence as if someone is watching over them.

In addition to Nurse Betty, there are numerous reports of other apparitions, including former patients who met tragic ends. The spirit of a young girl named "Emily" is frequently mentioned. Emily was a patient who supposedly died under mysterious circumstances. Her ghost is often seen in the children's ward, where she is said to play with toys and hum lullabies. Investigators have captured EVPs (electronic voice phenomena) that they believe to be Emily's voice, calling out for her mother or asking for help.

One of the more disturbing stories involves the spirit of a man known as "John." John was a violent patient who allegedly died during a struggle with the asylum's staff. His spirit is said to be particularly malevolent, often manifesting as a dark shadow that induces feelings of fear and aggression in those who encounter it. Visitors have reported sudden, overwhelming feelings of anger or dread when near the area where John is believed to have died. Some have even claimed to feel an invisible force pushing or shoving them.

The former operating rooms are another hotspot for paranormal activity. These rooms, once used for lobotomies and other invasive procedures, have a particularly dark history. Visitors have reported hearing the sounds of surgical instruments clattering and the faint screams of patients. The oppressive atmosphere in these rooms is palpable, and many who enter feel an immediate sense of unease. Paranormal investigators have captured numerous EVPs in this area, with voices pleading for help or crying out in pain.

The asylum's basement, which housed the morgue, is considered by many to be the most haunted part of the building. The cold, dark environment, combined with the knowledge of its past use, creates a terrifying experience for those who venture down there. Reports of ghostly apparitions, unexplained noises, and sudden drops in temperature are common. Some have seen shadowy figures moving among the old storage rooms, while others have heard the sound of gurneys being wheeled down the halls.

The Sheboygan Asylum has also been the site of numerous paranormal investigations by professional ghost hunters. These investigations have yielded a wealth of evidence supporting the claims of hauntings. Thermal cameras have captured inexplicable cold spots, often in the shape of human figures. EMF (electromagnetic field) detectors have recorded spikes in areas with no electrical sources, suggesting the presence of supernatural entities. Infrared cameras have captured images of shadowy figures and orbs of light moving through the building.

One particularly compelling piece of evidence was captured by a team using a spirit box, a device that scans radio frequencies to allow spirits to communicate. During a session in the basement, the investigators asked if anyone was present. The spirit box responded with a clear "Yes." When asked for a name, the device replied, "Emily," followed by, "Help me." This interaction, along with other findings, has convinced many that the Sheboygan Asylum is indeed haunted.

The stories and experiences from the Sheboygan Asylum have cemented its reputation as one of Wisconsin's most haunted locations. Despite its closure, the building continues to draw attention from those interested in the paranormal. For some, the hauntings are a reminder of the asylum's dark past and the suffering of its former residents. For others, they offer a glimpse into the unknown, providing evidence that life continues in some form beyond death.

The Sheboygan Asylum's haunted history is a testament to the enduring impact of its past. The spirits said to inhabit the building serve as a reminder of the lives once lived there and the stories that continue to unfold in the shadows. Whether one believes in ghosts or not, the tales of the Sheboygan Asylum offer a fascinating look into the mysteries of the supernatural and the ways in which history can linger long after the final chapter has been written.

The Sheboygan Asylum

# CHAPTER 8

## THE KARSTEN HOTEL

### (Kewaunee)

The Karsten Hotel in Kewaunee, Wisconsin, is a historic establishment that has long been associated with tales of the supernatural. Built in 1912 by William Karsten, this grand hotel has been the focal point of many ghost stories and paranormal investigations. Its rich history, combined with its vintage architecture and the numerous reports of ghostly encounters, make the Karsten Hotel a fascinating case for those interested in the paranormal.

William Karsten, the hotel's founder, was a prominent figure in Kewaunee's history. He envisioned the hotel as a luxury destination for travellers and a cornerstone of the community. Over the decades, the Karsten Hotel became known for its elegance and charm, attracting guests from all walks of life. However, with its age and storied past, it also accumulated a reputation for being haunted.

One of the most famous spirits said to haunt the Karsten Hotel is that of Agnes Karsten, William's niece. Agnes was known for her kindness and generosity, often helping to run the hotel and ensuring guests were well cared for. She lived at the hotel for many years until her untimely death in the 1940s. Guests and staff have reported seeing her apparition throughout the building, particularly in her former room, which is now known as Room 310. Agnes's ghost is described as a friendly presence, often seen in a blue dress, and she is known to interact with guests by turning lights on and off, opening doors, and even tucking people into bed.

Another well-known spirit is that of Billy Karsten, William's son. Billy lived in the hotel as a child and tragically died in a car accident in the 1930s. His playful spirit is said to linger in the hotel, particularly in the basement and the kitchen areas. Staff and guests have reported hearing the sound of a child's laughter and footsteps running through the halls. Objects are often found moved or misplaced as if Billy is still playing pranks from beyond the grave.

The third prominent ghostly figure associated with the Karsten Hotel is that of the former maintenance man, who is often referred to as "Howard." Howard worked at the hotel for many years and was known for his dedication to the upkeep of the building. He is believed to have died in the hotel, and his spirit is said to still roam the halls, particularly in the basement and the boiler room. Guests and staff have reported feeling an unexplainable chill in these areas, and tools and equipment are often found in places where they were not left. Howard's presence is generally perceived as watchful and protective as if he is still looking after the hotel.

In addition to these specific spirits, there are numerous reports of other unexplained phenomena throughout the Karsten Hotel. Guests have reported hearing disembodied voices, particularly in the hallways and common areas. These voices often sound like conversations or whispers, and they are most commonly heard late at night. Some guests have also reported hearing the sound of a piano playing in the lobby, even though the piano is no longer there.

Paranormal investigators who have visited the Karsten Hotel have captured a variety of evidence supporting the claims of hauntings. EVPs (electronic voice phenomena) have been recorded in several rooms, with voices responding to questions or calling out names. Thermal cameras have detected cold spots and anomalies that cannot be explained by natural causes. EMF (electromagnetic field) detectors have shown spikes in areas with no electrical sources, suggesting the presence of supernatural entities.

One particularly compelling investigation was conducted by the Wisconsin Paranormal Research Team (WPRT). During their investigation, the team set up equipment in various hotspots within the hotel, including Room 310, the basement, and the kitchen. They captured numerous EVPs with voices that seemed to correspond to the known spirits of Agnes, Billy, and Howard. In Room 310, the team captured an EVP of a woman's voice saying, "Hello," and another saying, "I'm here." In the basement, they recorded the sound of a child laughing, which they believe to be Billy's spirit.

The WPRT team also used a spirit box, a device that scans radio frequencies to allow spirits to communicate during their investigation. In the lobby, they asked if any spirits were present and received a clear response of "Yes." When asked for a name, the spirit box replied, "Agnes." The team felt a sudden drop in temperature, and one investigator reported feeling a gentle touch on her shoulder as if someone was trying to comfort her.

Guests who have stayed at the Karsten Hotel often leave with stories of their own paranormal experiences. Some have reported waking up in the middle of the night to find their belongings moved or the sensation of being watched. Others have described seeing shadowy figures in their rooms or hearing unexplained noises. Despite these eerie encounters, many guests report feeling a sense of warmth and hospitality, as if the spirits are simply part of the hotel's charm.

The Karsten Hotel's hauntings have not deterred visitors; in fact, they have become a significant draw for those interested in the paranormal. The hotel embraces its haunted reputation, offering ghost tours and paranormal investigation nights. These events allow guests to explore the hotel's haunted history and experience the supernatural phenomena for themselves. The hotel's staff are well-versed in the ghostly legends and are happy to share their own experiences and stories with curious guests.

The hauntings of the Karsten Hotel add a layer of intrigue and mystery to this historic establishment. The spirits of Agnes, Billy, Howard, and others who have passed through the hotel's doors seem to continue their connection to the place, creating an atmosphere that is both eerie and enchanting. Whether one is a sceptic or a believer, the stories of the Karsten Hotel's hauntings offer a fascinating glimpse into the unknown and a reminder that history often leaves an indelible mark on the places we inhabit.

In conclusion, the Karsten Hotel in Kewaunee, Wisconsin, stands as a testament to the enduring presence of the past. Its hauntings, steeped in history and personal tragedy, continue to captivate and mystify those who visit. The stories of Agnes, Billy, and Howard, along with the many other unexplained occurrences, create an aura of mystery that is impossible to ignore. For those seeking an encounter with the supernatural, the Karsten Hotel offers an experience that is both chilling and unforgettable.

The Kersten Hotel

# CHAPTER 9

## THE WAUSHARA HISTORICAL SOCIETY MUSEUM & OLD JAIL

### (Wautoma)

The Waushara County Historical Museum and Old Jail in Wautoma, Wisconsin, is a fascinating place steeped in history and mystery. This historic site, which once served as the county jail, has become the focal point of numerous ghost stories and paranormal investigations. The museum is not just a repository of the county's past; it is also said to be haunted by the spirits of infamous figures such as Ed Gein and his mother, Augusta.

The Waushara County Historical Museum, formerly the county jail, dates back to the early 20th century. This imposing structure, built in the classic architectural style of the time, once housed prisoners and served as the sheriff's residence. Over the years, it has seen its share of tragic events, crimes, and notorious inmates. Among the most infamous of these was Ed Gein, the notorious murderer and body snatcher whose gruesome crimes inspired several horror films, including "Psycho" and "The Texas Chainsaw Massacre."

Ed Gein was arrested in 1957 for the murder of Bernice Worden, a local hardware store owner. Upon his arrest, authorities discovered a house of horrors at his farm in Plainfield, Wisconsin. Gein had exhumed corpses from local graveyards and fashioned macabre trophies and keepsakes from their bones and skin. The shocking nature of his crimes sent waves of fear and revulsion through the community and beyond.

Following his arrest, Gein was held at the Waushara County Jail while awaiting trial. It is during this period that many believe his spirit became attached to the jail. According to local lore, the intense emotions and psychological turmoil Gein experienced while in custody may have left an indelible mark on the jail, leading to its current reputation as a haunted location.

Visitors and staff at the Waushara County Historical Museum have reported a wide range of paranormal activities over the years. These include inexplicable cold spots, disembodied voices, and shadowy figures seen roaming the halls. Some claim to have heard the sound of chains rattling and cell doors slamming shut despite the jail being long out of use. These eerie occurrences have been attributed to the restless spirit of Ed Gein.

One of the most common reports is the feeling of being watched, particularly in the areas where Gein was held. Some visitors have described an oppressive atmosphere as if the very air is thick with the weight of past horrors. Others have reported sudden drops in temperature, even on the warmest days, and the sensation of an unseen presence brushing against them.

Adding to the mystique of the museum is the alleged presence of Gein's mother, Augusta. Augusta Gein was a domineering and deeply religious woman who had a profound influence on her son. She instilled in him a fear of women and a belief that they were instruments of sin. Many believe that her strict and puritanical upbringing played a significant role in shaping Ed Gein's disturbed psyche.

Some paranormal enthusiasts speculate that Augusta's spirit may have followed her son to the Waushara County Jail, either out of a sense of protectiveness or to continue exerting her control over him even in death. Reports of her presence are often associated with a strong scent of roses, which was her favourite flower. Visitors have also claimed to hear a woman's voice reciting prayers or singing hymns, a chilling reminder of Augusta's influence on her son's twisted mind.

The Waushara County Historical Museum has become a popular destination for paranormal investigators. Teams equipped with various ghost-hunting tools such as EMF detectors, digital voice recorders, and thermal cameras have conducted numerous investigations within its walls. These investigations have yielded intriguing, if not outright chilling, results.

One notable investigation was conducted by the Wisconsin Paranormal Research Society (WPRS). During their visit, the team set up equipment in several hotspots, including the cells where Gein was held and the former sheriff's residence. They captured multiple EVPs (electronic voice phenomena) that seemed to respond to their questions. One particularly disturbing EVP recorded a voice whispering, "Help me," which some believe could be Gein's spirit seeking redemption or release from his torment.

The WPRS team also reported capturing unexplained shadows on their thermal cameras and experiencing sudden drops in temperature in areas where Gein's presence was most strongly felt. These findings, while not definitive proof of the supernatural, add to the growing body of evidence suggesting that the Waushara County Historical Museum and Old Jail may indeed be haunted.

Despite the dark history and the tales of hauntings, the museum serves an important role in preserving the history of Waushara County. It offers a glimpse into the past, showcasing artefacts, photographs, and exhibits that tell the story of the community and its evolution over the years. The staff, while respectful of the ghostly legends, remain committed to their mission of education and preservation.

For those intrigued by the paranormal, the Waushara County Historical Museum offers ghost tours and events that delve into the building's haunted history. These tours provide a unique opportunity to explore the jail after dark, hear firsthand accounts of ghostly encounters, and perhaps even experience something otherworldly.

In addition to the legends surrounding Ed Gein and his mother, the museum is also said to be haunted by other spirits from its time as a functioning jail. Former inmates who met tragic ends, whether through execution, suicide, or violent confrontations, are believed to linger within its walls. These restless spirits are thought to manifest in various ways, from eerie sounds and disembodied voices to full-bodied apparitions.

One particularly chilling tale involves the ghost of a former inmate who was executed in jail. Visitors have reported seeing a shadowy figure hanging from the ceiling in one of the cells, only for it to vanish when approached. The sound of muffled sobs and whispered pleas for mercy have also been heard in this area, adding to the building's eerie atmosphere.

The Waushara County Historical Museum and Old Jail stand as a testament to the darker chapters of the area's history. While the stories of hauntings and ghostly encounters may be unsettling, they also serve to remind us of the human lives and experiences that have shaped the region. Whether one is a sceptic or a believer, the museum offers a compelling and thought-provoking exploration of the past, where history and the supernatural intersect.

In conclusion, the Waushara County Historical Museum and Old Jail in Wautoma, Wisconsin, is a place where history and legend intertwine. The tales of hauntings, particularly those involving Ed Gein and his mother, Augusta, have captivated the imaginations of many. The museum, with its rich history and ghostly legends, continues to draw visitors and paranormal investigators alike, each hoping to catch a glimpse of the otherworldly. As the stories continue to be told and new experiences are added to the lore, the Waushara County Historical Museum remains a hauntingly fascinating destination.

The Waushara Historical Museum

# CHAPTER 10

## THE EAGLES CLUB

### (Milwaukee)

The Eagles Club in Milwaukee, Wisconsin, is an architectural marvel with a storied history that has both delighted and haunted its visitors. Located at 2401 W. Wisconsin Avenue, this majestic building, known officially as The Rave/Eagles Club, has been a centre for social gatherings, concerts, and community events since its inception. However, alongside its rich cultural heritage, the club is also reputed to be one of the most haunted places in Milwaukee, with numerous reports of ghostly encounters and paranormal activities that have captivated the imaginations of locals and paranormal enthusiasts alike.

Constructed in 1926 by the Fraternal Order of Eagles, the Eagles Club was originally designed to serve as a meeting hall and social club for its members. The building's grandeur, with its opulent ballroom, swimming pool, gymnasium, and multiple event spaces, made it a central hub for social activities in Milwaukee. Over the years, it has hosted countless events, including dances, banquets, and concerts, making it an integral part of the city's cultural fabric.

Despite its vibrant history, the Eagles Club has long been associated with tales of the supernatural. The building's labyrinthine corridors, hidden passageways, and expansive spaces create an eerie atmosphere, particularly when the venue is quiet and empty. Many of the ghost stories that surround the Eagles Club are rooted in its long history and the countless people who have passed through its doors, some of whom are believed to have never left.

One of the most frequently reported hauntings is that of a young girl who is often seen and heard near the swimming pool area. Witnesses have described seeing her ghostly figure standing by the edge of the pool or wandering through the hallways nearby. She is often seen wearing a vintage bathing suit, suggesting she may be from an earlier era. The girl is said to be playful and mischievous, with reports of her giggling and splashing water when no one else is around. Some believe she may have drowned in the pool, though historical records do not confirm this.

Another well-known spirit is that of a janitor who allegedly died in the building. Staff members and visitors have reported seeing a shadowy figure in janitorial attire, particularly in the basement and maintenance areas. This apparition is often seen carrying cleaning supplies and moving through the halls with a sense of purpose. Those who have encountered him describe an overwhelming feeling of sadness and loneliness as if the spirit is still diligently carrying out his duties even in death.

The ballroom, one of the most stunning features of the Eagles Club, is also said to be haunted. Many guests have reported seeing spectral figures dancing gracefully across the floor during quiet hours. These apparitions are often dressed in formal attire from various eras, adding to the timeless and otherworldly feel of the space. The ghostly dancers are sometimes accompanied by the faint strains of music, even when the room is silent and empty.

One particularly chilling account involves a man in a tuxedo who has been seen standing at the edge of the ballroom, watching the spectral dancers with a forlorn expression. Witnesses have described feeling a sudden drop in temperature and an overwhelming sense of melancholy when he appears. Some speculate that he may have lost a loved one at a dance or event held in the ballroom and is now forever trapped in a state of mourning.

The Eagles Club's basement, with its network of tunnels and hidden rooms, is perhaps the most unnerving part of the building. This area, which once housed a speakeasy during Prohibition, is rife with reports of paranormal activity. Visitors have reported hearing disembodied voices, footsteps, and the clinking of glasses as if the long-gone patrons of the speakeasy are still enjoying their clandestine gatherings. The basement's dark and damp environment only adds to the sense of foreboding that pervades the space.

Paranormal investigators who have explored the basement have captured numerous EVPs (electronic voice phenomena), which seem to corroborate the reports of ghostly activity. One particularly eerie recording captured a voice whispering, "Get out," while another picked up the sound of a glass breaking, followed by laughter. These recordings, along with the many eyewitness accounts, have cemented the basement's reputation as a hotspot for supernatural encounters.

The Eagles Club's gymnasium, with its towering ceilings and expansive floor space, is another area where ghostly sightings have been reported. Visitors have claimed to see shadowy figures moving through the gym, often appearing and disappearing without a trace. The sounds of basketballs bouncing and the echo of footsteps have been heard when the gym is empty, leading some to believe that the spirits of past athletes and club members still linger in the space.

One of the more unsettling reports involves the apparition of a man in athletic gear who is seen running laps around the gym. Witnesses have described him as appearing intensely focused, oblivious to the living, as he continues his ghostly exercise routine. This spirit is often accompanied by the sound of heavy breathing and the distinct squeak of sneakers on the gym floor, creating an eerie and surreal experience for those who encounter him.

The Eagles Club's ornate lobby and grand staircase are also said to be haunted. Visitors have reported seeing a well-dressed woman descending the staircase only to vanish before reaching the bottom. She is often described as wearing a vintage gown, and her presence is accompanied by a strong scent of perfume. This apparition is thought to be the spirit of a former club member or guest who frequented the building during its heyday.

In addition to these specific hauntings, there are numerous accounts of general paranormal activity throughout the Eagles Club. Lights are flickering on and off, doors opening and closing by themselves, and sudden temperature drops are common occurrences reported by staff and visitors alike. The building's extensive history and the countless events it has hosted seem to have left an indelible mark, creating an environment ripe for ghostly encounters.

The Eagles Club's reputation as a haunted location has attracted the attention of paranormal enthusiasts and investigators from across the country. Many have conducted investigations and tours, hoping to capture evidence of the supernatural. These efforts have yielded a wealth of photographs, recordings, and personal experiences that continue to fuel the building's haunted legend.

Despite the eerie tales and ghostly encounters, the Eagles Club remains a beloved and vibrant part of Milwaukee's cultural scene. Its rich history, stunning architecture, and role as a venue for music and events ensure that it continues to be a focal point for the community. The stories of hauntings only add to its mystique, drawing in curious visitors and paranormal enthusiasts eager to experience the building's unique atmosphere for themselves.

In conclusion, the Eagles Club in Milwaukee, Wisconsin, is a place where history and the supernatural intertwine. From the playful spirit of a young girl by the pool to the sorrowful ghost of a tuxedoed man in the ballroom, the building is home to a diverse array of paranormal activity. Whether one is a sceptic or a believer, the Eagles Club offers a fascinating glimpse into the past, where the echoes of history and the whispers of the beyond create an n unforgettable experience.

# CHAPTER 11

## BLOODY BRIDE BRIDGE

### (Stevens Point)

Bloody Bride Bridge, located in Stevens Point, Wisconsin, is an infamous local landmark known for its chilling ghost story. Nestled along County Highway HH, the bridge has become a magnet for paranormal enthusiasts, thrill-seekers, and curious visitors. The tale of the Bloody Bride is one that has been passed down through generations, growing more spine-tingling with each retelling. This story, which centres around a tragic accident and the ghostly apparition of a bride, has cemented the bridge's reputation as one of Wisconsin's most haunted sites.

The legend of Bloody Bride Bridge begins with a tragic wedding night. According to the most popular version of the story, a newlywed couple was driving home from their wedding reception late at night. As they crossed the bridge, their car veered off the road and crashed, resulting in the bride's death. Some say the groom survived, while others claim he perished alongside his bride. The specifics of the accident vary, but the core of the story remains the same: a young bride lost her life on what should have been the happiest night of her life.

In the years following the accident, reports of ghostly sightings began to emerge. The most common encounter involves the apparition of the bride herself. Witnesses have described seeing a spectral figure in a white wedding gown standing on the bridge or appearing suddenly in the middle of the road. Drivers have reported swerving to avoid hitting her, only to find that she has vanished into thin air. This phenomenon has led to many near-accidents and a pervasive sense of unease among those who travel the bridge at night.

Another variation of the legend involves the bride appearing in the backseat of a car as it crosses the bridge. This chilling encounter often begins with the driver noticing a strange presence or catching a glimpse of something in the rearview mirror. Upon turning around, they are met with the sight of the ghostly bride, her eyes staring blankly ahead. In some accounts, she disappears as soon as the car reaches the other side of the bridge, leaving the occupants shaken and terrified.

The haunting of Bloody Bride Bridge is not limited to visual sightings. Many people have reported hearing eerie sounds as they cross the bridge, especially at night. These sounds include the faint strains of wedding music, the soft rustling of a wedding dress, and the heart-wrenching sobs of a grieving bride. These auditory experiences add another layer of terror to the legend, making it one of the most comprehensive and compelling ghost stories in the region.

Paranormal investigators have taken a keen interest in Bloody Bride Bridge, conducting numerous investigations in an attempt to capture evidence of the supernatural. These investigations have yielded a variety of findings, including EVPs (electronic voice phenomena), mysterious light anomalies, and unexplained temperature fluctuations. Some investigators have even reported feeling a sudden, overwhelming sense of sadness or dread while on the bridge, which they attribute to the lingering presence of the bride's spirit.

One particularly compelling piece of evidence comes from a photograph taken by a local resident. The image, which has been widely circulated and analyzed, appears to show a faint, ghostly figure in a white dress standing on the bridge. Sceptics have argued that the photo could be a result of light reflection or camera malfunction, but many believe it to be genuine proof of the bride's haunting presence.

The bridge's eerie reputation has made it a popular destination for local ghost tours and paranormal events. These tours often include a visit to the bridge at night, where guides share the story of the Bloody Bride and encourage participants to watch for any signs of the supernatural. The tours have become a staple of Stevens Point's local lore, drawing both believers and sceptics eager to experience the bridge's haunted history firsthand.

Despite the fear and fascination surrounding Bloody Bride Bridge, it remains a functional part of the local infrastructure. Residents of Stevens Point cross it daily, some with a casual indifference to its haunted reputation, while others quicken their pace, eager to reach the other side. The bridge serves as a constant reminder of the area's rich tapestry of folklore and the enduring power of ghost stories.

The legend of the Bloody Bride has also had a significant impact on the local community, influencing everything from Halloween traditions to local art and literature. Every October, the bridge becomes a focal point for ghost hunters and thrill-seekers looking to experience a genuine scare. Local artists have created paintings and drawings inspired by the haunting, capturing the spectral beauty of the bride and the eerie ambience of the bridge. Writers and poets have penned stories and verses about the tragic tale, adding their own unique twists to the legend.

Despite the widespread acceptance of the legend, some sceptics dismiss the ghost stories as mere folklore or urban legend. They argue that the sightings and experiences can be attributed to psychological factors, such as the power of suggestion or the human tendency to see patterns and faces in random stimuli (a phenomenon known as pareidolia). These sceptics often point to the lack of concrete historical records detailing the supposed accident as evidence that the story is more myth than reality.

However, even the most ardent sceptics cannot deny the profound impact that the legend of Bloody Bride Bridge has had on the community. Whether one believes in the supernatural or not, the story serves as a potent reminder of the fragility of life and the enduring nature of love and loss. It is a tale that continues to captivate and terrify, drawing people to the bridge in search of a brush with the unknown.

In recent years, the legend has found new life on the internet, where forums, blogs, and social media posts have brought the story to a global audience. Paranormal enthusiasts from around the world share their experiences and theories, adding new layers of intrigue to the tale. This digital age of storytelling has only enhanced the bridge's haunted reputation, ensuring that the legend of the Bloody Bride will continue to thrive for generations to come.

In conclusion, Bloody Bride Bridge in Stevens Point, Wisconsin, is a site steeped in tragedy and mystery. The legend of the ghostly bride, with its heart-wrenching tale of love and loss, has captivated the imaginations of locals and visitors alike. From chilling visual sightings to eerie sounds and compelling pieces of evidence, the haunting of Bloody Bride Bridge is one of Wisconsin's most enduring and fascinating ghost stories. Whether one approaches the bridge with a sense of scepticism or a belief in the supernatural, the legend serves as a powerful testament to the enduring nature of folklore and the human fascination with the unknown.

Bloody Bride Bridge

# CHAPTER 12

## THE OCTAGON HOUSE

### (Fond Du Lac)

The Octagon House in Fond du Lac, Wisconsin, stands as a historical and architectural marvel with a reputation for being one of the most haunted places in the state. Built in the mid-19th century, the house's unique eight-sided design is a rare architectural gem. However, it is not just the structure that draws people to it; the tales of ghostly encounters and paranormal activity have made the Octagon House a focal point for ghost hunters and paranormal enthusiasts alike.

Constructed in 1856 by Isaac Brown, the Octagon House was part of a brief architectural trend inspired by Orson Squire Fowler, who believed that octagonal homes were healthier and more efficient than traditional designs. The house, with its 32 rooms spread across four floors, features high ceilings, large windows, and a central spiral staircase that ascends through the middle of the home. This layout allows for abundant natural light and ventilation, which were thought to promote good health. Despite its initial promise, the house has since become better known for its eerie atmosphere and unexplained phenomena.

The stories of hauntings at the Octagon House are numerous and varied, spanning over a century of paranormal reports. One of the most frequently mentioned spirits is that of Isaac Brown himself. Visitors and staff have reported seeing the figure of a man dressed in 19th-century attire roaming the halls and rooms of the house. This apparition is often described as being somewhat friendly, though his sudden appearances have startled many. Some believe that Brown's spirit remains in the house because of his deep attachment to the unique structure he created.

Another well-known ghost is that of a young girl who is believed to have died in the house under mysterious circumstances. This child spirit is often seen in the upper floors, particularly in what was once a nursery. Witnesses have reported hearing the sound of a child's laughter, the patter of small footsteps, and even the sound of a child crying. These occurrences are often accompanied by cold spots and an overwhelming sense of sadness as if the young spirit is still seeking comfort.

The basement of the Octagon House is also a hotspot for paranormal activity. Many visitors report feeling an oppressive presence and a sudden drop in temperature upon entering the basement. Shadows have been seen moving in the corners of the room, and unexplained noises, such as footsteps and the sound of objects being moved, are commonly reported. Some believe that the basement may have been used for purposes that were less than savoury, possibly even as a place for illicit activities during the Prohibition era, which could explain the uneasy energy that lingers there.

One of the most chilling stories involves the ghost of a woman in white who is said to wander the grounds of the Octagon House. She is often seen from a distance, appearing to glide effortlessly across the lawn before disappearing into thin air. This spectral figure is thought to be the spirit of a former resident or possibly a guest who met an untimely death on the property. Her appearances are usually accompanied by a feeling of melancholy and an unexplained fog that seems to settle around the area where she is seen.

The kitchen area of the house has its own set of ghostly occurrences. Objects have been known to move on their own, and utensils are found scattered in the morning despite being neatly put away the night before. Some visitors have reported hearing the sounds of a meal being prepared, complete with the clatter of pots and pans and the smell of cooking food, even though the kitchen is completely empty. These phenomena are thought to be the work of a former housekeeper or cook who continues to tend to her duties in the afterlife.

One of the more disturbing reports involves the feeling of being watched or even followed by an unseen entity. Many visitors have described the sensation of eyes upon them, particularly when they are alone in a room or walking down a hallway. This presence is often accompanied by an intense feeling of dread or anxiety, leading some to believe that not all of the spirits in the Octagon House are benign.

The paranormal activity at the Octagon House has attracted the attention of numerous ghost hunters and paranormal investigators over the years. Many of these investigators have captured compelling evidence of the hauntings, including EVPs (electronic voice phenomena), mysterious light anomalies, and unexplainable changes in temperature. Some have even recorded full-body apparitions and shadow figures on camera. These findings have only added to the house's reputation as a hotspot for supernatural activity.

Despite its haunted reputation, the Octagon House is also a cherished historical landmark in Fond du Lac. The local historical society has worked diligently to preserve the house and its contents, offering tours that educate visitors about the history and architectural significance of the building. However, it is often the ghost stories that draw the largest crowds, eager to experience the paranormal for themselves.

In recent years, the Octagon House has been featured in several paranormal television shows and documentaries, further cementing its status as one of Wisconsin's most haunted locations. These programs often highlight the house's rich history and the numerous ghostly encounters reported by visitors and staff. Each new investigation seems to uncover additional layers of mystery and intrigue, ensuring that the legend of the Octagon House continues to grow.

While some sceptics may dismiss the stories as mere folklore or the product of overactive imaginations, the sheer volume of reports and the consistency of the experiences suggest that there is something genuinely unexplainable happening at the Octagon House. Whether one believes in ghosts or not, the tales of hauntings at this historic home provide a fascinating glimpse into the supernatural and the enduring power of local legend.

In conclusion, the Octagon House in Fond du Lac, Wisconsin, is a place where history and the supernatural intersect. The unique architecture and rich history of the house provide a compelling backdrop for the numerous ghost stories and paranormal encounters reported by visitors and investigators alike. From the friendly spirit of Isaac Brown to the chilling presence in the basement, the Octagon House offers a wide range of ghostly experiences that continue to captivate and terrify those who dare to enter. Whether you visit for the history, the architecture, or the chance to encounter a ghost, the Octagon House promises an unforgettable experience that will leave you questioning the boundary between the living and the dead.

The Octagon House

# CHAPTER 13

## DARTFORD CEMETERY

### (Green Lake)

Dartford Cemetery in Green Lake, Wisconsin, is one of the state's most infamous haunted locations. With its picturesque setting and historical significance, the cemetery draws visitors interested in both its beauty and its eerie reputation. Many believe that Dartford Cemetery is a hotspot for paranormal activity, with numerous reports of ghostly sightings, unexplained phenomena, and eerie encounters that have persisted over the years. This 1000-word exploration delves into the history of Dartford Cemetery, the most well-known ghost stories associated with it, and the experiences of those who have dared to visit after dark.

## The History of Dartford Cemetery

Dartford Cemetery, located in the small town of Green Lake, was established in the mid-19th century. It serves as the final resting place for many of the area's earliest settlers, including prominent families and Civil War veterans. The cemetery's serene landscape, with its rolling hills, ancient trees, and meticulously maintained grounds, provides a peaceful resting place for those interred there. However, beneath this tranquil exterior lies a history rich with tales of tragedy and unexplained occurrences.

## Notable Ghost Stories and Paranormal Encounters

### The Wandering Spirits

One of the most commonly reported phenomena at Dartford Cemetery is the appearance of wandering spirits. Visitors have claimed to see ghostly figures roaming the grounds, especially during the twilight hours. These apparitions are often described as wearing clothing from different historical periods, suggesting they may be the restless spirits of those buried in the cemetery. The most frequent sightings occur near the older graves, where the headstones are weathered and moss-covered, adding to the eerie atmosphere.

### The Weeping Woman

A particularly chilling legend involves the spirit of a woman who is often seen weeping near a specific grave. According to local lore, she is the ghost of a young mother who died tragically, leaving behind a child. Witnesses report hearing the sound of soft sobbing, and some have even seen the spectral figure kneeling by the grave, her face buried in her hands. Attempts to approach her result in her sudden disappearance, leaving only the lingering sound of her sorrowful cries.

## The Children's Laughter

Another unsettling phenomenon at Dartford Cemetery is the sound of children's laughter echoing through the air. Despite the absence of any living children, visitors frequently hear the unmistakable sound of playful giggles, often near the graves of children who died in the 19th and early 20th centuries. Some have even reported seeing the apparitions of young children playing among the headstones, only to vanish when approached.

## The Phantom Caretaker

A ghostly figure believed to be a former caretaker of the cemetery has also been spotted. This apparition is often seen tending to the graves as if continuing his duties in the afterlife. Witnesses describe him as an elderly man dressed in old-fashioned work clothes, sometimes carrying a lantern. He is said to appear particularly on misty nights, his lantern casting an eerie glow as he moves among the headstones. Those who have encountered him describe a feeling of calm, suggesting he means no harm and is merely dedicated to his eternal task.

## The Haunted Mausoleum

Dartford Cemetery is home to several mausoleums, but one in particular stands out for its paranormal activity. Visitors have reported strange noises coming from within, such as knocking, whispering, and even the sound of footsteps. Some have experienced a sudden drop in temperature upon approaching the mausoleum, accompanied by an overwhelming sense of dread. Those brave enough to peer inside have sometimes seen ghostly faces staring back at them, adding to the mausoleum's sinister reputation.

## Personal Accounts and Investigations

Over the years, many individuals and paranormal investigation teams have visited Dartford Cemetery to document the supernatural occurrences. Their findings have only added to the cemetery's haunted reputation.

## The Ghost Hunters

Several paranormal groups have conducted investigations at Dartford Cemetery, using a variety of equipment such as EMF meters, infrared cameras, and audio recorders. These investigations have yielded numerous pieces of evidence, including EVPs (electronic voice phenomena), unexplained temperature fluctuations, and photographic anomalies. One particularly compelling EVP captured the voice of a child saying, "Come play," which was recorded near the area where children's laughter is often heard.

## Personal Experiences

Many visitors to Dartford Cemetery have shared their personal experiences, adding to the growing body of anecdotal evidence. One common experience involves the sensation of being watched or followed. Visitors have reported feeling an unseen presence shadowing their movements, often accompanied by a sudden chill. Others have felt an inexplicable sense of sadness or unease, particularly near certain graves.

One chilling account comes from a group of teenagers who visited the cemetery on a dare. They reported seeing a glowing figure near one of the mausoleums. As they approached, the figure vanished, leaving them terrified and convinced they had encountered a ghost. Another visitor described feeling a cold hand touch her shoulder while she was photographing an old headstone. When she turned around, no one was there, but she captured an orb of light in her photo, which she believed was a manifestation of a spirit.

## The Psychic's Visit

A local psychic who visited Dartford Cemetery claimed to have communicated with several spirits. According to her, the cemetery is a focal point for spiritual energy, with many souls lingering due to unresolved issues or a strong attachment to the earthly realm. She identified several specific spirits, including a Civil War soldier who frequently patrols the grounds and a young girl who seeks companionship. Her visit provided a deeper understanding of the emotional energy present in the cemetery and the possible reasons for the hauntings.

## The Cultural Impact

The stories of hauntings at Dartford Cemetery have had a significant impact on the local community and beyond. The cemetery has become a popular destination for ghost hunters, paranormal enthusiasts, and curious visitors. Local businesses have capitalized on this interest, offering ghost tours and themed merchandise. The tales of Dartford Cemetery have also been featured in various media, including books, documentaries, and television shows, further cementing its status as one of Wisconsin's most haunted locations.

## CONCLUSION

Dartford Cemetery in Green Lake, Wisconsin, is a place where history and the supernatural intertwine. With its tranquil beauty and eerie atmosphere, it is a site that captivates both the living and the dead. The numerous reports of ghostly encounters, ranging from wandering spirits and weeping women to phantom caretakers and playful children, create a rich tapestry of paranormal activity that continues to fascinate and terrify. Whether you are a sceptic or a believer, a visit to Dartford Cemetery is sure to leave a lasting impression, reminding us of the thin veil that separates our world from the realm of the unknown.

Dartford Cemetery

# CHAPTER 14

## THE RED GYM

### (University Of Wisconsin Madison)

The Red Gym at the University of Wisconsin-Madison is a historic building with a rich past that is reputed to be one of the campus's most haunted locations. Known for its striking architecture and historical significance, the Red Gym has garnered a reputation for paranormal activity, attracting the interest of ghost hunters, students, and curious visitors alike. This exploration delves into the history of the Red Gym, the various ghost stories associated with it, and the experiences of those who have encountered unexplained phenomena within its walls.

## History of the Red Gym

The Red Gym, officially named the University of Wisconsin-Madison Armory and Gymnasium, was constructed in 1894. Its distinctive red brick façade and Romanesque Revival architecture make it a standout building on campus. Originally built as a military armoury and gymnasium, the Red Gym served multiple purposes over the years, including as a venue for physical education, social events, and administrative functions.

The building's history includes periods of transition and adaptation. During World War II, it was used for military training, and in the post-war years, it continued to serve as a recreational and academic space. Over time, the Red Gym became a focal point of campus life, hosting various events, classes, and meetings. Its long history and the countless individuals who have passed through its doors contribute to the building's ghostly reputation.

## Paranormal Activity and Ghost Stories
### The Mysterious Sounds

One of the most commonly reported phenomena in the Red Gym is the presence of mysterious sounds. Visitors and staff have frequently reported hearing unexplained noises, such as footsteps echoing through the empty hallways, doors creaking open and shut on their own, and distant voices speaking in hushed tones. These sounds often occur during late hours or when the building is unoccupied, adding to the eerie atmosphere.

The origin of these noises remains unknown, but some speculate that they may be the residual energy of past events or the spirits of individuals who once frequented the building. The sounds are particularly unsettling because they often seem to come from areas that are not easily accessible, such as locked rooms or unused sections of the building.

## The Ghost of the Soldier

One of the most intriguing ghost stories associated with the Red Gym involves the apparition of a soldier. According to local lore, the ghost is that of a young man who may have been a military trainee during World War II. Witnesses have described seeing a figure dressed in a vintage military uniform wandering through the gymnasium, particularly in the area where the armoury was once located.

This soldier is said to appear as a shadowy figure, often seen moving swiftly and disappearing as soon as he is noticed. Some have reported feeling an unexplained chill or a sense of being watched when encountering the ghost. The soldier's presence is believed to be linked to the building's military past, and his spectral appearances are thought to be a remnant of his time in the building.

## The Woman in White

Another well-known ghost story involves a spectral woman dressed in white. The "Woman in White" is said to roam the hallways of the Red Gym, especially in the areas near the old locker rooms and showers. Descriptions of her vary, but she is often described as a ghostly figure in an old-fashioned white dress.

Witnesses have reported seeing her gliding silently down the halls or standing by the windows, her presence accompanied by a sudden drop in temperature. Some believe that she may be a former employee or a student from the early days of the university, and her ghostly appearance is thought to be tied to tragic events or unresolved issues from her past.

## The Haunted Gymnasium

The gymnasium itself is a focal point for paranormal activity. Some have reported seeing strange shadows and figures moving across the floor, even when the space is completely empty. The basketball hoops and gym equipment are sometimes said to move or shift on their own, adding to the sense of unease.

The gymnasium's large, echoing space is also a prime location for unexplained noises, including the sound of bouncing balls, footsteps, and even the clanging of weights. These noises often occur when the building is closed or when no one should be using the gym. The eerie activity in this area is thought to be connected to the building's history as a place of physical training and exercise.

# Personal Accounts and Investigations
## Student Experiences

Many of the ghost stories associated with the Red Gym come from students who have experienced paranormal activity firsthand. Some have reported feeling a presence while studying or working late in the building. Others have shared stories of seeing apparitions or hearing unexplained sounds while walking through the empty hallways.

One notable account involves a group of students who were using the gym for a late-night study session. They reported seeing a shadowy figure moving across the floor and hearing the sound of footsteps approaching, only to find the area completely empty when they investigated. This experience left them with a lasting sense of unease and contributed to the building's reputation as a haunted location.

## Ghost Hunters and Paranormal Investigators

The Red Gym has attracted the attention of several ghost hunters and paranormal investigators. These investigations have sought to document the building's supernatural activity using various tools and techniques, such as EVP (electronic voice phenomena) recorders, thermal cameras, and motion detectors.

Some investigations have reported capturing unexplained voices and sounds on audio recordings, as well as detecting unusual temperature fluctuations. Photographic evidence has also been presented, showing orbs and anomalies that some interpret as ghostly manifestations. These findings have been used to support the claims of hauntings and contribute to the building's lore.

## The Impact on the Campus Community

The stories of hauntings at the Red Gym have had a significant impact on the campus community. The building's ghostly reputation has become part of its mystique, drawing interest from students, alumni, and visitors. Ghost tours and paranormal events are sometimes organized to explore the building's haunted history, and the tales of its apparitions continue to intrigue and captivate those who hear them.

For some, the ghost stories add a sense of excitement and curiosity to the university experience. For others, the tales of hauntings serve as a reminder of the building's long and storied past. Regardless of one's belief in the supernatural, the Red Gym remains a symbol of history and mystery, with its ghostly legends adding to its unique character.

# CONCLUSION

The Red Gym at the University of Wisconsin-Madison is a historic building with a reputation for paranormal activity. From the mysterious sounds and ghostly apparitions to the haunted gymnasium and the Woman in White, the Red Gym's ghost stories contribute to its enigmatic allure.

Whether one views these tales as genuine encounters with the supernatural or as intriguing elements of the building's history, they continue to fascinate and captivate those who experience them. As a place where the past and present intersect, the Red Gym stands as a testament to the enduring allure of ghostly legends and the mysteries that lie within.

# CHAPTER 15

## FOREST HOME CEMETERY

### (Milwaukee)

Forest Home Cemetery in Milwaukee, Wisconsin, is one of the city's oldest and most historically significant cemeteries. Established in 1850, it is renowned not only for its rich history and notable interments but also for its reputation as a site of paranormal activity. The cemetery's long history, coupled with its distinctive Gothic Revival architecture and the many intriguing stories associated with it, has contributed to its status as a reputedly haunted location. This exploration delves into the history of Forest Home Cemetery, the ghostly legends associated with it, and the experiences of those who have encountered unexplained phenomena within its grounds.

## History of Forest Home Cemetery

Forest Home Cemetery covers over 200 acres and is situated in the heart of Milwaukee. It was designed by the landscape architect Calvert Vaux, who was also known for his work on Central Park in New York City. The cemetery's design reflects the picturesque landscape style popular in the 19th century, with meandering pathways, rolling hills, and serene natural beauty.

Over the years, Forest Home Cemetery has become the final resting place for many prominent figures in Milwaukee's history. Among those interred are pioneers, industrialists, and influential community leaders, including the founder of Milwaukee, Solomon Juneau, and the brewer Frederick Pabst. The cemetery's historical significance and the numerous notable graves contribute to its reputation as a place of historical and supernatural intrigue.

## Paranormal Activity and Ghost Stories
### The Ghost of the Founder

One of the most well-known ghost stories associated with Forest Home Cemetery involves the ghost of Solomon Juneau, the founder of Milwaukee. Juneau's grave is located in the cemetery's prominent "Founders' Circle," a section dedicated to Milwaukee's early settlers. According to local lore, Juneau's spirit is said to linger near his final resting place, occasionally appearing to visitors as a shadowy figure or a misty apparition.

Witnesses have reported seeing a ghostly figure resembling Juneau near his grave, often accompanied by a sense of coldness or an unexplained drop in temperature. Some have claimed to hear whispers or faint voices when approaching his tombstone. The legend of Solomon Juneau's ghost adds a layer of historical depth to the cemetery's paranormal reputation, intertwining Milwaukee's early history with its spectral lore.

## The Haunted Mausoleum

Forest Home Cemetery is home to several grand mausoleums, including the impressive Kline Mausoleum, which is known for its elaborate architecture and ornate detailing. The Kline Mausoleum, in particular, has been the focus of numerous ghost stories. Visitors and paranormal investigators have reported experiencing strange phenomena near this mausoleum, including sudden drops in temperature, unexplained noises, and shadowy figures.

One of the most intriguing stories involves a group of visitors who claimed to have seen a figure moving within the mausoleum, even though the structure was locked and empty at the time. Others have reported hearing strange sounds, such as footsteps or whispers, coming from inside the mausoleum despite the lack of any visible source. These experiences contribute to the mausoleum's reputation as a hotspot for paranormal activity within the cemetery.

## The Apparition of the Young Girl

Another haunting tale from Forest Home Cemetery involves the apparition of a young girl. This story centres around a specific grave, believed to be that of a young child who passed away under tragic circumstances. Visitors to the cemetery have reported seeing the ghostly figure of a young girl dressed in old-fashioned clothing, often near her grave.

Witnesses have described seeing the girl as a fleeting, ethereal presence, sometimes accompanied by a sense of sorrow or melancholy. Some have claimed to hear the sound of a child's laughter or crying near the grave, adding to the eerie atmosphere. The ghostly girl's appearance is often linked to the emotional weight of her untimely death, and her presence is thought to be a residual imprint of her tragic past.

### The Phantom Procession

One of the most dramatic and mysterious stories associated with Forest Home Cemetery is the tale of the phantom procession. According to reports, a spectral parade of figures is said to appear on certain nights, moving silently through the cemetery in a line or procession. Witnesses have described seeing ghostly figures dressed in period clothing walking in solemn procession without making a sound.

The phantom procession is often associated with the cemetery's historical significance and the many funerals and memorial services that have taken place over the years. Some believe that the procession represents a lingering echo of past ceremonies or a manifestation of the grief and loss experienced by those who have been laid to rest at Forest Home. The appearance of the procession is said to be accompanied by a profound sense of solemnity and reverence.

## Personal Accounts and Investigations
### Experiences of Visitors

Numerous visitors to Forest Home Cemetery have shared their personal accounts of paranormal experiences. Some have reported feeling an unexplained presence or being followed by an unseen entity as they wandered through the cemetery. Others have recounted seeing shadowy figures or experiencing sudden, inexplicable cold spots.

One notable account involves a group of friends who visited the cemetery at night and claimed to have seen a ghostly figure standing near a grave. The figure reportedly disappeared when approached, leaving the witnesses with a lasting impression of the cemetery's eerie atmosphere. These personal experiences contribute to the cemetery's reputation as a haunted location and add to the overall sense of mystery surrounding Forest Home.

## Paranormal Investigations

Forest Home Cemetery has attracted the attention of various paranormal investigators and ghost hunters over the years. These investigations have sought to document the reported paranormal activity using a range of tools and techniques, such as EVP (electronic voice phenomena) recorders, thermal cameras, and motion detectors.

Some investigations have reported capturing unexplained voices or sounds on audio recordings, as well as detecting unusual temperature fluctuations in areas associated with paranormal activity. Photographic evidence has also been presented, showing orbs and anomalies that some interpret as ghostly manifestations. These findings have been used to support the claims of hauntings and contribute to the cemetery's ghostly lore.

## The Impact on the Community

The stories of hauntings at Forest Home Cemetery have had a significant impact on the local community and beyond. The cemetery's ghostly reputation has attracted interest from paranormal enthusiasts, historians, and curious visitors. Ghost tours and paranormal events are sometimes organized to explore the cemetery's haunted history, and the tales of its apparitions continue to captivate those who hear them.

For some, the ghost stories add an element of excitement and intrigue to the cemetery's historical significance. For others, the tales of hauntings serve as a reminder of the cemetery's role as a place of memory and reflection. Regardless of one's belief in the supernatural, Forest Home Cemetery remains a symbol of Milwaukee's history and a site of enduring mystery and fascination.

## CONCLUSION

Forest Home Cemetery in Milwaukee is a historic and culturally significant location with a reputation for paranormal activity. From the ghost of Solomon Juneau and the haunted mausoleum to the apparition of the young girl and the phantom procession, the cemetery's ghost stories contribute to its enigmatic allure. Whether one views these tales as genuine encounters with the supernatural or as intriguing elements of the building's history, they continue to fascinate and captivate those who experience them. As a place where the past and present intersect, Forest Home Cemetery stands as a testament to the enduring allure of ghostly legends and the mysteries that lie within.

Forest Home Cemetery

# CHAPTER 16

## THE OLD WADE HOUSE

### (Greenbush)

The Old Wade House in Greenbush, Wisconsin, is a historic landmark renowned for its intriguing past and reputed hauntings. Nestled in the picturesque Kettle Moraine State Forest, the Wade House has captivated the imagination of visitors and paranormal enthusiasts with its tales of spectral encounters. This exploration delves into the history of the Old Wade House, the ghostly legends associated with it, and the experiences of those who have encountered the supernatural within its walls.

### History of the Old Wade House

The Old Wade House, constructed in 1850, originally served as a stagecoach inn and a stopover for travellers journeying between Milwaukee and Fond du Lac. Built by the Wade family, the house quickly became a bustling hub for travellers, offering lodging, food, and rest to weary passengers. Its location along the old stagecoach route made it a key stop for those traversing the rugged terrain of early Wisconsin.

The Wade House is notable for its classic Greek Revival architectural style, characterized by its grand columns, wide verandas, and stately design. Over the years, it has been meticulously preserved and restored to reflect its 19th-century origins. Today, it operates as a historical site and museum, offering visitors a glimpse into life during the mid-19th century.

In addition to its historical significance, the Old Wade House has gained fame for its reputed hauntings, which have intrigued and spooked both staff and visitors alike.

## The Ghostly Legends of the Old Wade House
## The Tragic Deaths

One of the most enduring ghost stories associated with the Old Wade House involves tragic deaths that allegedly occurred on the property. According to local lore, there were several deaths at the inn, including those of children and travellers who passed away under mysterious or unfortunate circumstances. These deaths are said to have left residual energies that continue to manifest in the form of ghostly apparitions.

Witnesses have reported hearing the sound of children playing and laughing in empty rooms or hallways, often accompanied by the sight of shadowy figures. Some have claimed to see spectral figures of travellers or staff members moving about the inn as if reliving their final moments.

## The Ghost of Mrs Wade

The ghost of Mrs. Wade, the wife of the inn's original owner, is one of the most commonly reported apparitions at the Old Wade House. According to stories, Mrs. Wade was a beloved figure known for her hospitality and kindness. Her spirit is said to linger in the inn, continuing her duties of caring for guests even after her passing.

Visitors and staff have reported encountering a ghostly woman dressed in period clothing, often in the kitchen or dining areas. She is said to be seen preparing food or arranging the dining room, and her presence is often accompanied by the smell of freshly baked bread or other comforting scents. Some have even described feeling a gentle, reassuring touch or hearing soft, soothing voices when Mrs. Wade's ghost is near.

## The Phantom Stagecoach Driver

Another prominent ghostly figure associated with the Old Wade House is that of a phantom stagecoach driver. The stagecoach driver is believed to be a spectral representation of one of the many drivers who once passed through the inn. Witnesses have reported seeing a ghostly figure dressed in period attire, often near the old stagecoach route or within the grounds of the property.

The phantom stagecoach driver is said to appear as a shadowy figure or a misty presence, sometimes accompanied by the sound of clattering hooves or the distant rumble of a stagecoach. This apparition is often described as moving deliberately and purposefully as if continuing its journey along the old stagecoach route.

## The Haunting of the Old Dining Room

The Old Wade House's dining room is known for its eerie atmosphere and reported paranormal activity. Guests and staff have reported a range of unexplained phenomena in this area, including flickering lights, sudden drops in temperature, and the sound of unseen footsteps.

Some visitors have described feeling an oppressive or unsettling presence while dining or exploring the area, and some have claimed to see ghostly figures seated at the dining tables. The dining room is also associated with the ghostly laughter of children and the clinking of dishes and silverware, which seem to manifest without any apparent source.

## The Mystery of the Hidden Room

One of the most intriguing aspects of the Old Wade House is the mystery of a hidden room, which is said to be the site of several ghostly encounters. The hidden room, located in the attic or basement, is believed to have been used for storage or as a private retreat in the past.

Witnesses have reported hearing strange noises and encountering ghostly figures when exploring this area. Some have described seeing shadowy shapes or feeling an unexplained sense of foreboding while near the hidden room. The mystery surrounding the room's purpose and the nature of the apparitions associated with it adds an additional layer of intrigue to the ghost stories of the Old Wade House.

## Personal Accounts and Investigations
### Experiences of Visitors

Visitors to the Old Wade House have shared numerous personal accounts of paranormal experiences. Many have reported feeling a sense of being watched or followed, particularly in the inn's older sections. Some have described seeing apparitions or hearing unexplained noises, such as footsteps or whispers.

One notable account involves a visitor who claimed to have seen a ghostly figure standing in a doorway, only for the figure to vanish when approached. Others have reported feeling sudden cold spots or experiencing strange sensations, such as being touched or brushed by an unseen presence.

## Paranormal Investigations

The Old Wade House has attracted the attention of various paranormal investigators and ghost hunters over the years. These investigations have sought to document the reported paranormal activity using a range of tools and techniques, including EVP (electronic voice phenomena) recorders, infrared cameras, and motion detectors.

Some investigations have reported capturing unexplained voices or sounds on audio recordings, as well as detecting unusual temperature fluctuations in areas associated with paranormal activity. Photographic evidence has also been presented, showing orbs and anomalies that some interpret as ghostly manifestations. These findings have contributed to the ongoing fascination with the Old Wade House and its reputed hauntings.

## The Impact on the Community

The ghost stories and paranormal activity associated with the Old Wade House have had a significant impact on the local community and beyond. The tales of hauntings have attracted interest from paranormal enthusiasts, historians, and curious visitors. Ghost tours and paranormal events are sometimes organized to explore the inn's haunted history, and the stories of its apparitions continue to captivate those who hear them.

For some, the ghost stories add an element of excitement and intrigue to the historical significance of the Old Wade House. For others, the tales of hauntings serve as a reminder of the inn's rich history and the many lives that have touched its walls. Regardless of one's belief in the supernatural, the Old Wade House remains a symbol of Wisconsin's past and a site of enduring mystery and fascination.

## CONCLUSION

The Old Wade House in Greenbush, Wisconsin, is a historic and culturally significant location with a reputation for paranormal activity. From the tragic deaths and the ghost of Mrs. Wade to the phantom stagecoach driver and the haunting of the old dining room, the inn's ghost stories contribute to its enigmatic allure. Whether one views these tales as genuine encounters with the supernatural or as intriguing elements of the building's history, they continue to fascinate and captivate those who experience them. As a place where the past and present intersect, the Old Wade House stands as a testament to the enduring allure of ghostly legends and the mysteries that lie within.

The Wade House

# CHAPTER 17

## THE FIRST WARD SCHOOLHOUSE

### (Wisconsin Rapids)

Hauntings of the First Ward Schoolhouse in Wisconsin Rapids, Wisconsin

The First Ward Schoolhouse in Wisconsin Rapids, Wisconsin, is a historic building with a rich past and a reputation for being haunted. Built in the late 19th century, this schoolhouse has witnessed over a century of educational activities, community gatherings, and significant changes. Today, it is known not only for its historical value but also for its reputed paranormal activity, making it a point of interest for ghost enthusiasts and curious locals alike.

**Historical Background**

The First Ward Schoolhouse was established in 1898, serving as an educational institution for the children of Wisconsin Rapids. Designed in the architectural style of the period, the building features classic elements such as high ceilings, large windows, and sturdy brick construction. It was part of the broader movement in the late 19th and early 20th centuries to improve educational facilities across the United States, reflecting a growing emphasis on public education and community development.

Throughout its operational years, the First Ward Schoolhouse was a central hub for the local community. It not only provided education but also served as a venue for community events, meetings, and social gatherings. The schoolhouse continued to function as an educational facility until the 1970s when it was eventually closed and repurposed for various uses.

In the decades following its closure as a school, the building was utilized for different purposes, including as a community centre and a historical site. Its enduring presence in the community has made it a significant landmark, both historically and in the realm of paranormal lore.

## The Ghost Stories of the First Ward Schoolhouse
## The Apparition of the Old Teacher

One of the most frequently reported ghostly figures associated with the First Ward Schoolhouse is that of an elderly teacher. Witnesses have described encountering a spectral figure dressed in period-appropriate attire, often seen walking through the hallways or standing in the classroom areas. This apparition is believed to be the spirit of a former teacher who dedicated many years to educating the children of Wisconsin Rapids.

The teacher's ghost is often reported to be seen or heard in the late evening hours, and witnesses have described a feeling of calm and warmth associated with the apparition. Some have even claimed to receive a sense of reassurance or guidance from the ghost, which aligns with the teacher's nurturing and dedicated role during her lifetime.

## The Mysterious Disembodied Laughter

Another well-documented phenomenon at the First Ward Schoolhouse is the sound of disembodied laughter. Visitors and staff have reported hearing the distinct sound of children's laughter echoing through the building, even when the rooms are empty and no children are present. The laughter is often described as being joyful and playful, reminiscent of the sounds of children during recess or class activities.

The origins of this laughter are unknown, but some speculate that it may be connected to the many children who once attended the schoolhouse. The sound is particularly prominent in areas such as the old classrooms or the playground, where the echoes of past activities seem to linger.

## The Ghostly Footsteps

The phenomenon of unexplained footsteps is another commonly reported experience at the First Ward Schoolhouse. Visitors and staff have described hearing the sound of footsteps walking through the hallways, often when no one else is present in the building. The footsteps are sometimes heard pacing back and forth or moving up and down the stairs.

These footsteps are often accompanied by a sense of being watched or followed, adding to the eerie atmosphere of the building. Some witnesses have reported feeling cold spots or sudden changes in temperature in the areas where the footsteps are heard, which is commonly associated with paranormal activity.

## The Phantom Children

In addition to the sounds of disembodied laughter, several people have reported seeing ghostly figures of children within the First Ward Schoolhouse. These apparitions are said to appear as faint, shadowy forms or as more defined, childlike figures dressed in old-fashioned school attire. The sightings are often accompanied by an eerie feeling or a sense of nostalgia.

Witnesses have described seeing these phantom children playing in the hallways, sitting at desks, or peeking out from doorways. The presence of these ghostly figures is believed to be connected to the many students who once attended the school, and their continued presence in the building may reflect the fond memories or unresolved energies associated with their time there.

## The Haunting of the Library

The library area of the First Ward Schoolhouse is known for its particularly high level of reported paranormal activity. Visitors and staff have described seeing shadowy figures moving among the bookshelves, hearing the sound of pages turning, and experiencing sudden cold spots. The library's quiet and contemplative atmosphere seems to amplify the sense of unease and mystery.

Some have also reported encountering ghostly figures in the library, including a shadowy man who appears to be searching for a book or a lost item. The library's role as a repository of knowledge and its association with learning may contribute to the perceived presence of spirits still drawn to the intellectual and educational aspects of the building.

# Personal Accounts and Investigations
## Accounts from Visitors

Numerous personal accounts from visitors and staff provide insight into the haunting experiences at the First Ward Schoolhouse. Many have reported feeling an unexplained presence or encountering ghostly figures during their time in the building. Some have described feeling a sudden chill or an oppressive atmosphere in certain areas, particularly in the older parts of the schoolhouse.

One notable account involves a visitor who claimed to have seen a ghostly figure of a child standing at the top of the stairs. The figure reportedly vanished when approached, leaving the visitor with a sense of wonder and curiosity. Other visitors have reported hearing the sound of disembodied laughter while exploring the classrooms or hallways, adding to the building's mystique.

## Paranormal Investigations

The First Ward Schoolhouse has been the subject of various paranormal investigations over the years. These investigations have utilized a range of tools and techniques, including EVP (electronic voice phenomena) recorders, infrared cameras, and motion sensors, to document and analyze the reported ghostly activity.

Some investigations have yielded intriguing results, such as unexplained voices or sounds captured on audio recordings and anomalies detected by motion sensors. Photographic evidence has also been presented, showing orbs and other unexplained phenomena that some interpret as manifestations of spirits.

One particularly notable investigation involved a team of ghost hunters who spent an extended period in the building, capturing a series of unexplained events and anomalies. Their findings contributed to the ongoing fascination with the First Ward Schoolhouse and its reputation as a haunted location.

## The Impact on the Community

The ghost stories and paranormal activity associated with the First Ward Schoolhouse have had a significant impact on the local community and beyond. The building's haunted reputation has attracted interest from paranormal enthusiasts, historians, and curious visitors. Ghost tours and paranormal events are sometimes organized to explore the school's haunted history, and the stories of its apparitions continue to captivate those who hear them.

For some, the ghost stories add an element of excitement and intrigue to the historical significance of the First Ward Schoolhouse. For others, the tales of hauntings serve as a reminder of the building's rich history and the many lives that have touched its walls.

Regardless of one's belief in the supernatural, the First Ward Schoolhouse remains a symbol of Wisconsin Rapids' past and a site of enduring mystery and fascination.

## CONCLUSION

The First Ward Schoolhouse in Wisconsin Rapids, Wisconsin, is a historic and culturally significant location with a reputation for paranormal activity. From the ghostly apparitions of teachers and children to the sounds of disembodied laughter and phantom footsteps, the schoolhouse's ghost stories contribute to its enigmatic allure. Whether viewed as genuine encounters with the supernatural or as intriguing elements of the building's history, these tales continue to fascinate and captivate those who experience them. As a place where the past and present intersect, the First Ward Schoolhouse stands as a testament to the enduring allure of ghostly legends and the mysteries that lie within.

The First Ward School House

# CHAPTER 18

## THE HOAN BRIDGE

### (Milwaukee)

### The Haunting of Hoan Bridge: Milwaukee's Eerie Landmark

Nestled along the shores of Lake Michigan in Milwaukee, Wisconsin, the Hoan Bridge is more than just a vital transportation link; it's also a site of eerie legends and ghostly tales. Opened in 1977, this striking piece of infrastructure is known for its distinctive design and the role it plays in connecting downtown Milwaukee to the southern suburbs. However, beneath its imposing arches and across its sprawling lanes, the bridge is also shrouded in ghostly lore that has intrigued and unsettled locals and visitors alike.

## A Brief History of the Hoan Bridge

Before delving into the supernatural stories, it's essential to understand the Hoan Bridge's history. Named after the former Milwaukee mayor Daniel Hoan, the bridge is an architectural marvel featuring a distinctive cantilevered design that spans the Milwaukee River and Lake Michigan. The bridge is a crucial part of

Milwaukee's transportation infrastructure, providing a vital link between different parts of the city.

Despite its practical function, the Hoan Bridge has become a focal point for numerous ghost stories and paranormal experiences. The origins of these tales are as varied as the legends themselves, but they all share a common thread of eerie occurrences and unsettling encounters.

## The Legend of the Jumpers

One of the most prevalent and unsettling legends associated with the Hoan Bridge involves reports of individuals who have allegedly jumped from the bridge into the waters below. These stories have contributed to a growing belief that the bridge is haunted by the spirits of those who met a tragic end on or near the structure.

Witnesses have reported seeing ghostly figures leaping from the bridge, only for these apparitions to vanish before hitting the water. Some locals claim to have heard the sounds of splashing and cries for help despite there being no visible sign of an actual event. The stories of these apparitions often carry a sense of sadness and despair, reflecting the tragic nature of the supposed events.

## The Phantom Hitchhiker

Another haunting legend tied to the Hoan Bridge involves a mysterious hitchhiker who is said to appear on the bridge at night. According to local lore, this phantom hitchhiker is a spectral figure, often described as a young woman who is seen standing on the bridge's shoulder or near its entrance, seeking a ride.

Those who claim to have encountered this ghostly figure describe her as appearing out of nowhere, often in the middle of the night. The hitchhiker is said to vanish without a trace once a driver approaches or offers assistance. Some accounts even suggest that those who have picked her up experience unexplained disturbances or a sudden drop in temperature within their vehicle.

## Strange Sounds and Unexplained Noises

In addition to sightings of apparitions, the Hoan Bridge is also reputed to be a hotspot for strange sounds and unexplained noises. Visitors and passersby have reported hearing disembodied voices, footsteps, and other eerie sounds coming from the bridge, particularly during the night.

These sounds are often described as unsettling and disconcerting, contributing to the bridge's haunted reputation. The noises are sometimes attributed to the spirits of those who have died on the bridge or nearby, with some speculating that these sounds are the residual energy of tragic events that have occurred over the years.

## Paranormal Investigations and Eyewitness Accounts

The Hoan Bridge has attracted the attention of paranormal investigators and enthusiasts, who have conducted investigations to uncover evidence of ghostly activity. These investigations often involve the use of electronic equipment designed to detect unusual occurrences, such as EVP (electronic voice phenomenon) recordings and thermal imaging.

Some investigators have reported capturing unexplained phenomena, such as anomalous readings or unexplained fluctuations in temperature. These findings, coupled with numerous eyewitness accounts of ghostly sightings and eerie noises, contribute to the belief that the Hoan Bridge is a site of genuine paranormal activity.

Eyewitness accounts from locals and visitors further support the haunting claims. Many individuals have come forward with stories of unsettling experiences on the bridge, ranging from sightings of ghostly figures to strange noises and sudden feelings of dread. These personal accounts add to the bridge's mystique and contribute to its reputation as a haunted location.

## The Impact of Urban Legends and Media

The Hoan Bridge's reputation as a haunted location is also influenced by urban legends and media coverage. Stories of hauntings often gain traction through word of mouth, local folklore, and media portrayals, which can amplify existing beliefs and contribute to the perpetuation of ghostly legends.

In the case of the Hoan Bridge, media coverage of alleged ghost sightings and paranormal investigations has helped to cement its status as a haunted landmark. News stories, documentaries, and even local folklore have played a role in shaping public perceptions of the bridge and its supernatural associations.

## The Role of Tragic History and Folklore

The Hoan Bridge's haunted reputation is intertwined with the tragic history and folklore that surround it. The stories of ghostly apparitions, mysterious sounds, and paranormal encounters are often linked to the bridge's past and the broader historical context of the area.

For example, the stories of individuals jumping from the bridge and the phantom hitchhiker are often viewed through the lens of tragic events and local folklore. These narratives reflect broader themes of despair, loss, and the search for closure, which are common elements in ghost stories and paranormal legends.

## CONCLUSION

The Hoan Bridge in Milwaukee, Wisconsin, stands as a testament to the state's rich tapestry of haunted locations. Its striking architecture and vital role in the city's infrastructure make it an iconic landmark, while its reputation for ghostly activity adds an intriguing layer of mystery. The legends of ghostly jumpers, phantom hitchhikers, and unexplained noises contribute to the bridge's haunted reputation, drawing the curiosity of paranormal enthusiasts and visitors alike.

Whether driven by tragic events, cultural folklore, or the allure of the unknown, the Hoan Bridge's haunting stories continue to captivate and unsettle those who encounter them. As a focal point of ghostly legends and eerie encounters, the Hoan Bridge remains a significant part of Milwaukee's paranormal landscape, adding to the city's rich history of supernatural intrigue.

The Hoan Bridge

# CHAPTER 19

## THE MASONIC TEMPLE

### (Milwaukee)

The Haunting of the Masonic Temple in Milwaukee, Wisconsin

The Masonic Temple in Milwaukee, Wisconsin, stands as a grand monument to the city's architectural and historical heritage. With its majestic façade, intricate details, and storied past, the building has long been a significant landmark in Milwaukee's urban landscape. However, beyond its impressive exterior and historical significance, the Masonic Temple is also reputed to be one of Milwaukee's most haunted locations. The temple's haunting tales are intertwined with its history, and the eerie stories of ghostly apparitions and paranormal encounters have contributed to its reputation as a site of supernatural intrigue.

## A Brief History of the Masonic Temple

The Masonic Temple, located at 822 North Broadway Street, was constructed in 1927 and served as a central meeting place for the Freemasons of Milwaukee. The temple's design, crafted by the architectural firm of Herman E. T. Rohl, is an embodiment of

Beaux-Arts architecture, characterized by its grandiosity and ornate detailing. The building features a large central rotunda, elaborately decorated interiors, and a range of symbolic Masonic motifs.

Over the decades, the Masonic Temple has been a hub for various Masonic activities and gatherings, including ceremonial events, social functions, and community services. Its historical significance extends beyond its architectural beauty, as it has been a focal point for Milwaukee's Masonic community and a symbol of fraternal tradition.

## The Origins of the Haunting

The origins of the Masonic Temple's haunting are steeped in local lore and historical events. The building's grand and somewhat enigmatic atmosphere, combined with its long history, has fostered an environment ripe for ghost stories and supernatural speculation. Several factors contribute to the temple's reputation as a haunted site, including its historical significance, the nature of Masonic traditions, and the various accounts of paranormal activity reported by visitors and staff.

One theory suggests that the temple's association with secretive and ritualistic practices may contribute to its haunted reputation. The Freemasons are known for their esoteric traditions and ceremonies, which some believe could leave behind residual energy or attract supernatural entities. Additionally, the temple's long history and the various events that have taken place within its walls may have left an imprint on the building, contributing to its ghostly lore.

## Reports of Paranormal Activity

Numerous accounts of paranormal activity have been reported at the Masonic Temple over the years, adding to its reputation as a haunted location. These reports include sightings of ghostly apparitions, unexplained noises, and other eerie occurrences that have intrigued and unsettled those who have experienced them.

1. **Ghostly Apparitions**: One of the most commonly reported phenomena at the Masonic Temple is the sighting of ghostly apparitions. Witnesses have described seeing shadowy figures or transparent forms moving through the building, particularly in the areas associated with Masonic rituals and ceremonies. These apparitions are often reported to be dressed in period-appropriate attire, suggesting that they may be the spirits of individuals connected to the temple's history.

2. **Unexplained Noises**: Another frequent report involves unexplained noises within the temple. Visitors and staff have reported hearing disembodied footsteps, doors creaking open and closed, and distant conversations with no apparent source. These

sounds are often described as being particularly eerie and unsettling, contributing to the building's haunted atmosphere.

3. **Cold Spots and Temperature Fluctuations**: Cold spots and sudden temperature fluctuations are also commonly reported at the Masonic Temple. These phenomena are often associated with paranormal activity, as sudden temperature drops are believed to be indicative of the presence of supernatural entities. Witnesses have reported experiencing these cold spots in various parts of the building, including areas where ghostly apparitions have been sighted.

4. **Disembodied Voices**: Some reports include hearing disembodied voices or whispers within the temple. These voices are often described as being faint and indistinct, making it difficult for witnesses to discern their origins or content. The presence of these voices adds to the building's eerie reputation and contributes to the overall sense of unease experienced by those within its walls.

## The Role of Masonic Traditions

The Masonic Temple's association with Masonic traditions and rituals may play a role in its haunted reputation. The Freemasons are known for their complex and symbolic rituals, which some believe could leave behind residual energy or attract supernatural entities. The secrecy surrounding Masonic practices and the ceremonial nature of their meetings could contribute to the building's enigmatic atmosphere and its reputation as a site of paranormal activity.

Some theorists suggest that the rituals performed within the temple could create a form of energetic imprint, which may manifest as ghostly apparitions or unexplained phenomena. The combination of historical significance and ritualistic practices may contribute to the building's status as a haunted location.

## Paranormal Investigations

The Masonic Temple has attracted the attention of paranormal investigators and enthusiasts, who have conducted investigations to uncover evidence of ghostly activity. These investigations often involve the use of specialized equipment, such as EVP (electronic voice phenomenon) recorders, infrared cameras, and electromagnetic field (EMF) detectors.

Some investigators have reported capturing anomalous readings or unexplained phenomena during their investigations. These findings, coupled with numerous eyewitness accounts of ghostly sightings and eerie occurrences, contribute to the belief that the Masonic Temple is a site of genuine paranormal activity.

## The Influence of Urban Legends and Media

The Masonic Temple's haunted reputation is also influenced by urban legends and media portrayals. Stories of ghostly encounters and paranormal investigations often gain traction through word of mouth, local folklore, and media coverage. The media portrayal of haunted locations can amplify existing beliefs and contribute to the perpetuation of ghostly legends.

In the case of the Masonic Temple, media coverage and local legends have played a role in shaping public perceptions of the building and its supernatural associations. News stories, documentaries, and local folklore have helped to cement the temple's status as a haunted landmark and have contributed to the intrigue surrounding its ghostly tales.

## CONCLUSION

The Masonic Temple in Milwaukee, Wisconsin, stands as a testament to the city's architectural and historical heritage, but it is also a site of ghostly intrigue and supernatural speculation. The building's grand design, historical significance, and association with Masonic traditions have contributed to its reputation as a haunted location. Reports of ghostly apparitions, unexplained noises, and other eerie occurrences add to the temple's mystique and continue to captivate those interested in the paranormal.

Whether driven by historical events, Masonic traditions, or the allure of the unknown, the haunting stories associated with the Masonic Temple remain a significant part of Milwaukee's supernatural landscape. The building's ghostly tales and eerie occurrences contribute to its status as a haunted landmark and continue to fascinate and unsettle those who encounter it.

The Masonic Temple

# CHAPTER 20

## THE MILWAUKEE COURTHOUSE

### (MILWAUKEE)

### The Hauntings of the Milwaukee Courthouse

The Milwaukee Courthouse, officially known as the Milwaukee County Courthouse, is a historic landmark located in downtown Milwaukee, Wisconsin. This grand building, with its impressive architecture and significant role in the city's legal system, is also reputed to be one of Milwaukee's most haunted locations. The courthouse's long history, combined with its dramatic architecture and the serious nature of the proceedings that have taken place within its walls, has contributed to its reputation as a site of supernatural activity.

### A Brief History of the Milwaukee Courthouse

The Milwaukee County Courthouse, completed in 1929, is an architectural marvel designed by the prominent architect Eugene S. Richards. The building, which features a Beaux-Arts style with Renaissance Revival influences, boasts a striking facade, detailed ornamentation, and a distinctive clock tower. Its construction marked a significant expansion in the city's legal infrastructure and provided a grand setting for the administration of justice.

Over the decades, the courthouse has witnessed numerous legal proceedings, from high-profile trials to routine legal matters. It has been the backdrop for pivotal moments in Milwaukee's history, serving as a place where justice was administered and legal matters were resolved. The building's storied past, combined with its imposing and often sombre atmosphere, has made it a focal point for ghostly legends and paranormal speculation.

## The Origins of the Haunting

The origins of the Milwaukee Courthouse's haunting are intertwined with the building's history and the nature of the activities that have taken place within its walls. Some believe that the courthouse's association with legal disputes, trials, and high-stress situations may contribute to its reputation as a haunted location. The energy of intense legal battles, emotional courtroom dramas, and significant historical events may leave an imprint on the building, resulting in the ghostly phenomena reported by witnesses.

Additionally, the courthouse's architectural design, with its grandiose and sometimes intimidating features, may contribute to the building's eerie atmosphere. The combination of historical significance, dramatic architecture, and the nature of the activities conducted within the courthouse creates an environment that is ripe for supernatural speculation.

## Reports of Paranormal Activity

Numerous accounts of paranormal activity have been reported at the Milwaukee Courthouse, contributing to its reputation as a haunted location. These reports include sightings of ghostly apparitions, unexplained noises, and other eerie occurrences that have intrigued and unsettled those who have experienced them.

1. **Ghostly Apparitions**: One of the most frequently reported phenomena at the Milwaukee Courthouse is the sighting of ghostly apparitions. Witnesses have described seeing shadowy figures or transparent forms moving through the building, particularly in areas associated with intense legal proceedings or historical events. These apparitions are often reported to be dressed in period-appropriate attire, suggesting that they may be the spirits of individuals connected to the courthouse's history.

2. **Unexplained Noises**: Another common report involves unexplained noises within the courthouse. Visitors and staff have reported hearing disembodied footsteps, doors creaking open and closed, and distant conversations with no apparent source. These sounds are often described as being particularly eerie and unsettling, contributing to the building's haunted atmosphere.

3. **Cold Spots and Temperature Fluctuations**: Cold spots and sudden temperature fluctuations are also commonly reported at the Milwaukee Courthouse. Witnesses have experienced sudden drops in temperature or pockets of cold air in various parts of the building, including areas where ghostly apparitions have been sighted. These phenomena are often associated with paranormal activity and contribute to the overall sense of unease experienced by those within the courthouse.

4. **Elevator Malfunctions**: Some reports include strange malfunctions of the courthouse's elevators. Witnesses have described elevators behaving erratically, stopping at floors with no one present or moving on their own. These occurrences are often linked to ghostly activity and add to the building's reputation as a site of supernatural intrigue.

5. **Disembodied Voices**: Reports of disembodied voices or whispers are also common at the courthouse. These voices are often described as faint and indistinct, making it difficult for witnesses to discern their origins or content. The presence of these voices adds to the building's eerie reputation and contributes to the overall atmosphere of paranormal activity.

## The Influence of Historical Events

The Milwaukee Courthouse has been the site of numerous significant legal events and high-profile trials over the years. Some of these events, including controversial trials or cases involving serious criminal activity, may contribute to the building's haunted reputation. The energy and emotions associated with these events could potentially leave a residual imprint on the courthouse, resulting in the ghostly phenomena reported by witnesses.

Additionally, the courthouse has served as a backdrop for various historical moments, including political events, social changes, and legal battles. The building's role in these significant events may contribute to its status as a haunted location, with the spirits of those connected to these moments potentially lingering within its walls.

## Paranormal Investigations

The Milwaukee Courthouse has attracted the attention of paranormal investigators and enthusiasts who have sought to uncover evidence of ghostly activity. These investigations often involve the use of specialized equipment, such as EVP (electronic voice phenomenon) recorders, infrared cameras, and electromagnetic field (EMF) detectors.

Some investigators have reported capturing anomalous readings or unexplained phenomena during their investigations. These findings, coupled with numerous eyewitness accounts of ghostly sightings and eerie occurrences, contribute to the belief that the Milwaukee Courthouse is a site of genuine paranormal activity.

## The Role of Urban Legends and Media

The courthouse's haunted reputation is also influenced by urban legends and media portrayals. Stories of ghostly encounters and paranormal investigations often gain traction through local folklore, news coverage, and popular media. The media portrayal of haunted locations can amplify existing beliefs and contribute to the perpetuation of ghostly legends.

In the case of the Milwaukee Courthouse, media coverage, and local legends have played a role in shaping public perceptions of the building and its supernatural associations. News stories, documentaries, and local folklore have helped to cement the courthouse's status as a haunted landmark and have contributed to the intrigue surrounding its ghostly tales.

## CONCLUSION

The Milwaukee County Courthouse stands as a testament to the city's architectural and legal history, but it is also a site of ghostly intrigue and supernatural speculation. The building's grand design, historical significance, and the intense nature of the legal proceedings that have taken place within its walls have contributed to its reputation as a haunted location.

Reports of ghostly apparitions, unexplained noises, and other eerie occurrences add to the courthouse's mystique and continue to captivate those interested in the paranormal. Whether driven by historical events, architectural design, or the allure of the unknown, the haunting stories associated with the Milwaukee Courthouse remain a significant part of the city's supernatural landscape. The building's ghostly tales and eerie phenomena contribute to its status as a haunted landmark and continue to fascinate and unsettle those who encounter it.

The Milwaukee Courthouse

# CHAPTER 21

## BROADHEAD MANOR

### (BROADHEAD)

The Haunting of Broadhead Manor, Broadhead, Wisconsin

Nestled in the quaint town of Broadhead, Wisconsin, Broadhead Manor is an imposing structure with a history as rich and layered as its ornate architecture. This stately mansion, once a symbol of prosperity and grandeur, is now notorious for its eerie reputation and ghostly tales. Its haunted legacy, fueled by a blend of historical events, architectural features, and local legends, has made it a focal point of paranormal interest and supernatural speculation.

### Historical Background

Broadhead Manor, built in the early 20th century, is a prime example of the opulent residential architecture of its time. Designed in the Colonial Revival style, the manor boasts expansive interiors, intricate woodwork, and stately furnishings. The mansion was originally constructed by a wealthy local businessman, whose family enjoyed the home for several decades before its use shifted over time.

The manor's history includes various functions beyond its role as a family residence. At different points, it has served as a private club, a guesthouse, and a community centre. Each of these phases brought its own set of events and activities, contributing to the rich tapestry of stories associated with the manor.

## The Origins of the Haunting

The origins of Broadhead Manor's haunting are deeply intertwined with its history. As with many historic buildings, the manor's past is marked by a series of events and circumstances that may have left an imprint on its environment. These include personal tragedies, significant life changes, and the day-to-day experiences of its occupants.

One of the primary sources of the manor's ghostly reputation stems from the untimely and tragic deaths that have occurred within its walls. Historical accounts and local legends suggest that several individuals associated with the manor met with misfortune, and their unresolved fates may contribute to the building's supernatural aura.

# REPORTS OF PARANORMAL ACTIVITY

Reports of paranormal activity at Broadhead Manor are both numerous and varied, encompassing a range of ghostly phenomena that have intrigued and unsettled those who have encountered them. The following are some of the most frequently reported occurrences:

1. **Apparitions**: Perhaps the most commonly reported phenomenon is the sighting of apparitions. Witnesses have described seeing ghostly figures dressed in period clothing, believed to be former occupants or visitors to the manor. These apparitions are often seen in various rooms of the mansion, including the grand staircase, the library, and the dining hall. Some reports suggest that these figures may be engaged in activities reflective of their lives, such as reading or conversing, adding a layer of depth to their ghostly presence.

2. **Unexplained Noises**: Another frequent report involves unexplained noises within the manor. Visitors and staff have reported hearing footsteps, doors creaking, and faint whispers or conversations without a discernible source. These sounds often occur in areas where no one else is present, contributing to the eerie atmosphere and fueling speculation about the manor's haunted nature.

3. **Cold Spots and Temperature Fluctuations**: Cold spots and sudden temperature changes are commonly experienced at

Broadhead Manor. Witnesses have reported encountering unexplained drops in temperature or areas of the building that feel unnaturally cold, even when the rest of the space is warm. These phenomena are often associated with paranormal activity and are thought to be indicative of a ghostly presence.

4. **Flickering Lights and Electrical Malfunctions**: Reports of flickering lights and electrical malfunctions are also prevalent. Witnesses have described lights turning on and off by themselves, appliances behaving erratically, and other electrical disturbances. These occurrences are often attributed to the influence of spirits or other supernatural forces.

5. **Mysterious Shadows and Movements**: Some visitors have reported seeing mysterious shadows or movements out of the corner of their eyes. These shadows are often described as shifting or moving in ways that defy natural explanation. Such sightings contribute to the building's haunted reputation and add to the sense of unease experienced by those within the manor.

## Influence of Historical Events

The history of Broadhead Manor is marked by a series of events that may contribute to its haunted reputation. Among these are personal tragedies, such as untimely deaths or unresolved disputes, that may have left a lingering impact on the building. Local legends and folklore also play a role in shaping the manor's ghostly reputation, with stories of tragic events and unresolved mysteries adding to the intrigue.

One particularly notable event in the manor's history is the sudden and unexpected death of a former resident who passed away under mysterious circumstances. The unresolved nature of this death and the emotional turmoil associated with it may contribute to the haunting phenomena reported by witnesses. Additionally, the manor's use as a community centre and guesthouse may have brought a variety of individuals through its doors, each potentially leaving their own imprint on the building.

## Paranormal Investigations

The haunting of Broadhead Manor has attracted the attention of paranormal investigators and enthusiasts seeking to uncover evidence of ghostly activity. Investigations at the manor often involve the use of specialized equipment, such as EVP (electronic voice phenomenon) recorders, infrared cameras, and electromagnetic field (EMF) detectors.

Some investigators have reported capturing anomalous readings or unexplained phenomena during their investigations. These findings, coupled with the numerous eyewitness accounts of ghostly encounters and eerie occurrences, contribute to the belief that Broadhead Manor is a site of genuine paranormal activity.

## Local Legends and Urban Myths

Local legends and urban myths play a significant role in shaping the haunted reputation of Broadhead Manor. Stories passed down through generations often highlight the most dramatic or unsettling aspects of the manor's history, contributing to its supernatural allure.

One popular legend involves the ghost of a young woman who is said to roam the halls of the manor, seeking something or someone she left behind. Another legend tells of a former resident who met a tragic end and now lingers in the manor, unable to find peace. These stories, while not always substantiated by concrete evidence, contribute to the building's haunted reputation and fuel the imagination of those who hear them.

## Cultural Impact and Media Portrayals

The haunted reputation of Broadhead Manor has been further amplified by its portrayal in local media and popular culture. Stories of ghostly encounters and paranormal investigations have been featured in news articles, documentaries, and other media outlets, helping to cement the manor's status as a haunted landmark.

Media portrayals often focus on the most dramatic and unsettling aspects of the manor's ghostly reputation, contributing to the building's allure and intrigue. These portrayals help to perpetuate the legends and myths surrounding the manor, adding to its mystique and appeal.

## CONCLUSION

Broadhead Manor, with its rich history and architectural grandeur, is a focal point of supernatural speculation and ghostly legends in Broadhead, Wisconsin. The building's haunted reputation, fueled by reports of apparitions, unexplained noises, and other eerie phenomena, has captivated the imagination of those who have encountered its ghostly presence.

The manor's history, including personal tragedies and significant events, contributes to its reputation as a haunted location. Whether driven by historical events, architectural features, or local legends, the haunting stories associated with Broadhead Manor continue to intrigue and unsettle those who experience them.

As a site of paranormal interest, Broadhead Manor remains a testament to the enduring allure of the supernatural and the enduring fascination with ghostly legends. The building's ghostly tales and eerie occurrences contribute to its status as a haunted landmark, ensuring that its haunting legacy endures for years to come.

Broadhead Manor

# ABOUT THE AUTHOR

 Scott E. Bowser is the author of three non-fiction books, Gein (2021), The Travelers Guide to Ed Gein (2021), and The Ed Gein Chronicles (2023). Scott appeared on the MGM Plus TV show "Psyco: The Lost Tapes of Ed Gein."

Scott was born in 1964 in Kingsford, Michigan, and lived his young years in Neenah, Wisconsin. Scott always had an interest in true crime and the paranormal, whether it be reading about it or watching it on TV.

Scott now lives in Wisconsin Rapids. Wisconsin, where, in his spare time, he gives Ed Gein tours in Plainfield, Wisconsin. Scott also, in his spare time, creates children's and adult coloring books, which are also available on Amazon. He is currently writing a screenplay for his first book "Gein."

## OTHER BOOKS BY SCOTT BOWSER

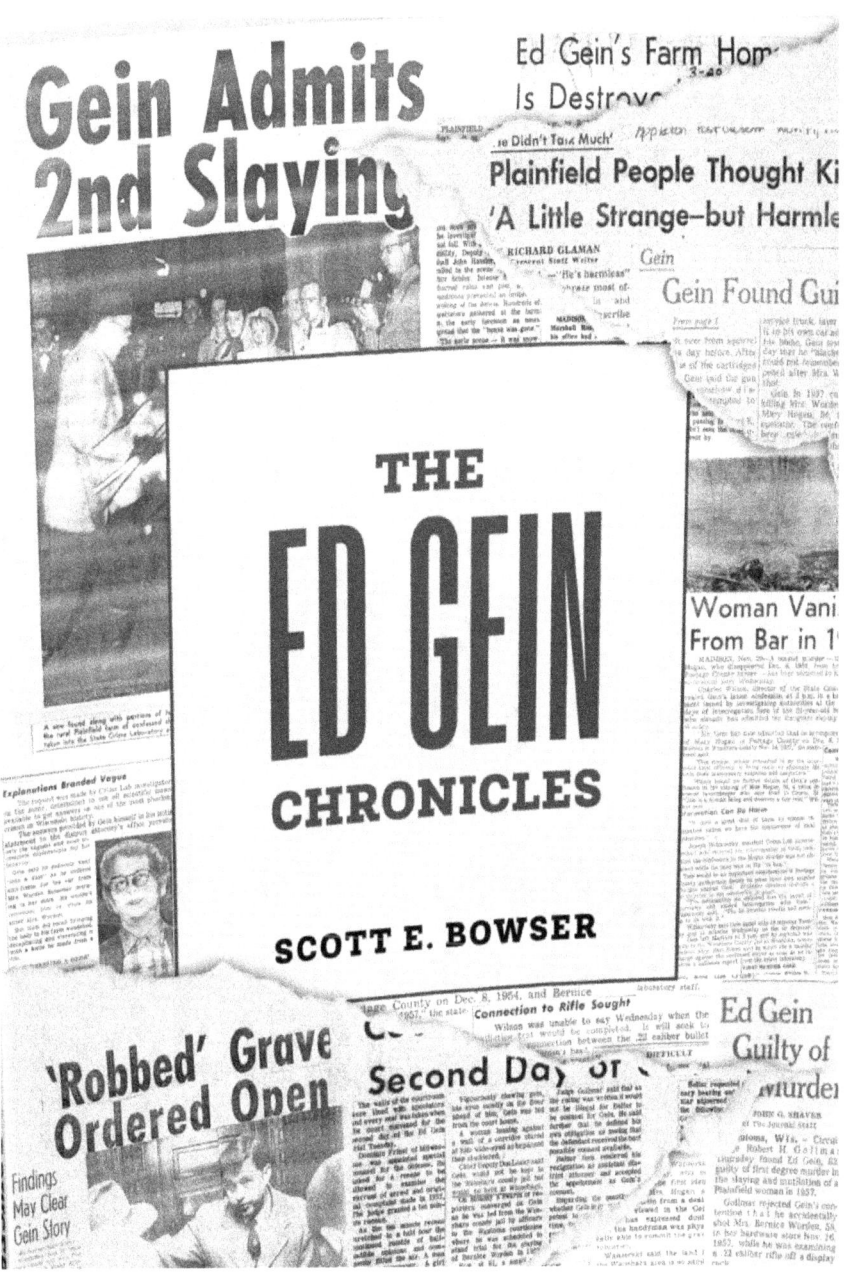

www.ingramcontent.com/pod-product-compliance
Lightning Source LLC
LaVergne TN
LVHW012022060526
838201LV00061B/4420